HOW TO BE AN EFFECTIVE CHURCH WOMAN

BOOKS BY CAROLYN P. BLACKWOOD
Published by The Westminster Press

How to Be an Effective Church Woman
The Pastor's Wife

How to Be
an Effective
Church Woman

by
CAROLYN P. BLACKWOOD

With an Introduction by
ANDREW W. BLACKWOOD

Philadelphia
THE WESTMINSTER PRESS

DEDICATED
to the
Laywoman in the Home Church

ACKNOWLEDGMENTS

I wish to express deep gratitude:

To Dr. Paul Meacham and his associates in The Westminster Press, for their patience in waiting for a manuscript long delayed.

To my many friends, both pastors and laywomen, who responded fully to the questionnaires I sent them; also to the groups of women before whom I have spoken.

To many individuals: my beloved cousin, Mary Wilson Abbott, my nurse and companion through five weary months of being confined to bed and wheel chair; Alice Smith Harper, our former church secretary; our cousin, Elizabeth Watterson Carnes; my sister, Grace Philips Easter; Margaret Beebe Niles, who was my pastor's wife through seventeen beautiful years; and others who made generous contributions of material. Also to my sister-in-law, Rose Blackwood, for typing the first draft of the manuscript; to my son James, for making valuable suggestions; and to his secretary, Gwen Wright, for the final typing.

Especially do I owe a lasting debt of gratitude to my husband for tender nursing during my illness, for constant encouragement which kept me from despair, for fetching and carrying books from the library, and for countless other ministries. I cannot estimate how much I owe him.

Most of all, my deep gratitude to the Heavenly Father for answering the prayers of hosts of friends, which have brought me both healing and strength.

CAROLYN PHILIPS BLACKWOOD.

Wynnewood, Pennsylvania,
Spring, 1955.

CONTENTS

INTRODUCTION

This book deals with the laywoman as member, worker, and leader in the local church. Mrs. Blackwood looks on the home church as the most important place in any community, except the Christian home. She regards the church woman as the most distinctive gift of American Protestantism to the world today. The author does not long for the time when women will displace men as church leaders, either in the pulpit or elsewhere. Still she feels that the work of church women ought to receive far more recognition than it now gets from us men, and that in the church of tomorrow both men and women should work together according to the spirit and the teachings of the New Testament about equality between the two sexes.

Kindly and clearly the book shows the contributions and the attainments of the church woman, with much about her problems in the changing church of today, and her opportunities for still larger service in the morrow. The problems range all the way from the needs of the Negro neighbors across the street to the place of missions in a world twice cursed by global war, and now full of fears. The discussion centers round the home church, but the horizon broadens so as to reach out to the ends of the earth. The stress falls on one woman at a time, but there is increasing emphasis on the call for leadership and teamwork, all for the sake of the Kingdom.

Mrs. Blackwood has found this book harder to write than the former one, *The Pastor's Wife*. There the author worked in a field where others had led the way; here she has had to blaze her own trail. In books she has found little on her subject, except in denominational publica-

tions. In a certain yearbook, typical of many, she counted
187 pages about the activities and the achievements of
men, with only one page about the work of women, and
that page devoid of facts. Worse still, soon after she started
to dig she fell and broke her hip. Soon she discovered that
the new " stake in the flesh " interfered with the spirit of
joyous adventure, and interrupted the flow of ink from
her pen.

The resulting book has come out of much tribulation.
It may also cause searchings of heart. Out of rich and
varied experiences as a church woman the writer has come
to certain convictions, some of which run counter to present trends. In every such case she wishes the reader to
search the Scriptures — especially the book of The Acts
— in the spirit of prayer, and then to reach a decision at
the foot of the cross. Mrs. Blackwood writes as a Christian
optimist. She believes in the church woman of today, and
expects still more from her daughters in the morrow.

Best of all, the writer keeps pointing to the Source of all
wisdom and strength. In churches large, small, and of
medium size, while serving in the ranks or as a leader of
other women, she has learned to rely on strength not her
own. While she sets the standards high, and keeps them
on a lofty Christian level, she also makes clear how to find
grace in every hour of need. Meantime she does not bid
the reader envision herself as a would-be martyr, but as
" a perfect woman, nobly planned, to warn, to comfort,
and command "; and yet " a creature not too bright or
good for human nature's daily food." This kind of church
woman ought gladly to say with the apostle, " I can do all
things in him who strengthens me " (Phil. 4:13, R.S.V.).

ANDREW W. BLACKWOOD.

I

THE WORK OF THE CHURCH WOMAN

1

AS A GRATEFUL PROTESTANT

Stand fast therefore in the liberty
wherewith Christ hath made us free.
— Gal. 5:1.

W ILL YOU MAKE a talk at our Catholic Women's Communion Breakfast?" The question came over the
telephone, and I did not know what to reply. "Libby, you
seem to forget that I am a Protestant." "No, indeed! That's
why we want you to make this talk. We have just started
laywomen's work in our parish, and we want you to help
us do it better."

A few weeks later at a Roman Catholic church in one
of our suburbs, sixty-seven women arrived in a hard rain.
After they had taken Communion in the church they went
to a nearby hotel for breakfast, with a Protestant woman
as speaker. She began by thanking the priest, the only man
present. She told him she would have brought him a gift
of her book, *The Pastor's Wife,* if she had thought it would
do him any good. He threw back his head and roared, and
the women joined in his mirth. At the end of the meeting
the priest thanked the speaker for what she had said about
the Christian home. He told her he hoped she would
come back someday. It was a heart-warming morning.

This experience opened my eyes. It made me see as
never before that as a Protestant girl and woman I had
always enjoyed privileges and opportunities not open to
my sisters in the Roman Catholic Church, or even to many
Protestant women in Great Britain and on the Continent.

I had simply taken for granted my Christian liberty and all my church work. When I began to investigate, I found that nowhere else in the world and at no other time in history have women and girls had the freedom of opportunity for Christian usefulness that we Protestant women enjoy in the United States.

The women of the Roman Catholic Church are beginning to have a hunger for such privileges. In order to keep away from controversy I shall say nothing more about that. I am glad to know that the women members of Protestant churches across the Atlantic are getting larger opportunities for the kind of work they can do better than their menfolk. Think of Hungary, for example. During the German invasion, all the men and boys were under arms. The women and children, huddled in cellars, engaged in searching their souls in earnest prayer. The women vowed to God that if they came out alive they would give themselves to a more spiritual service. After the siege was lifted, those women felt eager to express their new faith, but they discovered that some pastors did not go along with lay activity on the part of women. It seems, however, that, like the widow in Luke 18:3, they kept " troubling " the pastors until they finally consented to let the women have their way.

" In the tremendous fact of a resurgent laity," writes President John A. Mackay, of Princeton Seminary, " the Reformation doctrine of the universal priesthood of all believers is being carried forward to a new and needed expression. The Reformers of the sixteenth century meant by this doctrine that all Christians, however humble, have the right to approach the throne of Deity by the sole mediation of Jesus Christ. But the doctrine came to be interpreted all too exclusively in terms of the spiritual *privi-*

leges of believers. The one-sidedness in the interpretation of this great evangelical truth is now being rectified. Christian lay people, men and women, are awakening to the fact that they have equal *responsibility* with the clergy to serve Christ and his Church according to their time and talents." ("Report to the Church," *Presbyterian Life,* May 13, 1954.)

Men took the leadership in the Protestant Reformation of the sixteenth century. Of course women like Martin Luther's wife, Katharina von Bora, kept house behind the scenes. But if Martin jokingly referred to his wife as "my rib," he just as often called her "my lord." (See Roland Bainton's discussion of Luther's marriage and home life in *Here I Stand,* chapter XVII.) Her influence was real yet indirect. Others did as Martin's "Katie" did — they left the leadership in the hands of men. Although there are some exceptions, it has remained with men ever since. But in our country women and their children have found a remarkable freedom. When the history of American Protestantism is written, the chief contribution of our people to the vitality of the Kingdom may well be the work of laywomen in congregations and in the larger branches of the Church.

Enjoying Equality with Men

Here in America we Protestant women realize what the apostle meant in his "Epistle of Christian Freedom": "There is neither male nor female; for ye are all one in Christ Jesus" (Gal. 3:28). Most Jewish men no longer repeat the prayer that still appears in some of their authorized books of devotion: "Blessed art Thou, O Lord, our God, who hast not made me a woman." At least unofficially, Protestant women have at long last won equality of church standing with their husbands, brothers, and sons, though sometimes we are staggered by the lack of recognition. Of course we trust that our names are written in heaven. We expect to hear our Master say, " Well done." Yet we wonder about page four of the typical church bulletin. If it must have a printed list of officers, why do most of them have to be men?

In May, 1952, the Board of Managers of the United Church Women made a study of " The Service and Status of Women in the Churches." A questionnaire was sent to sixteen denominations, which enroll twenty-five million members — almost half the Protestants in the nation. The questionnaire was limited to two areas: participation of women in policy-making, and the ordination of women to the ministry. Most of the replies from churches that exclude women from authoritative bodies admit that there is no constitutional or doctrinal reason for this attitude, but they submit quite a list of nontheological factors against women's participation in this work, such as: " Tradition supports the idea that men run the church on all levels "; " Men feel freer when women aren't there "; " Women prefer to have men make the decisions," etc.

On the other hand, where women have been permitted to serve on official boards, the report is that they have carried out their assignments on a very high plane of efficiency and devotion. There is now a definite trend toward increasing the number of women in the work of boards and committees, but the feeling is strong that they should be chosen because of their ability and not because they are women.

The Rural Department of Drew Seminary, Madison, New Jersey, made a recent survey which covered six southeastern states. The investigators found that men hold three times as many offices as women, but the women are doing twice as much work. Men professed to be willing to work but no one was asking them. The pastors know that they can depend on the women when there is something to be done.

In a congregation we know, the women do at least twice as much work as the men, and do it better, but the list of church officers follows the old political slogan of " sixteen to one." Does this mean that it takes forty-eight men to do as much as three women? Three times a year, in this particular church, the male officers are solemnly inducted into service, and their wives sit back and watch. Since the men make the plans for these public meetings, they might be amazed to hear what the women say about them! Why do they practically ignore the women's work? We can listen and hear the same question repeated in larger assemblies of a certain denomination, where, as far as public recognition goes, women and children are still " to be seen and not heard."

Making a Distinct Contribution

Before I started to write this book I sent out questionnaires on the subject of the contribution of women to the work of the Church. One set went to laywomen of various denominations in large and small churches, both in city and in rural areas. The other questionnaire went to ministers in all sorts of churches, though not to pastors of the congregations to which these laywomen belong. Both questionnaires brought quick replies. The answers are full of enthusiasm for the work being done by women, and fairly swarm with practical ideas, many of which will appear on later pages. These replies impress me. All through the years I have taken part in church work, as a pastor's wife and later as a laywoman, and I have paid special attention to the contributions by women. Still I can't get over the amount and variety of work reported by the women and praised by the ministers.

The pastors seem to be one hundred per cent in support of an idea we women have held for a long time, that the Kingdom program of any local church, and of every Protestant denomination, depends mostly on women. One minister declares: "We simply could not do the great work we are doing in this church if it were not for the women." Another pastor was called upon by some members of his official board, who suggested that he should have an assistant. He was surprised, and answered, "I have three hundred assistants in the women of this church." Dozens of other pastors write about the large and unique contribution by women, and almost every man gives different reasons for his gratitude.

Some pastors in large churches, however, notice a tendency among lay people to let down in their activities. "The attitude is that the minister and the staff are here to carry on the Lord's work, and that the lay folk are here to support and enjoy it. This is getting away from our Protestant heritage. We therefore are trying to develop a plan by which lay folk will take back the home church and make it their own. The ministry is here simply in an advisory capacity, to recruit, train, inspire, and lead the laity in the performance of the Church's function, both in the community and in the world. It will take time, but our people are beginning to get the idea."

These conditions will be found among men, I believe, more frequently than among women. Nevertheless we know that we have scarcely touched the fringes of what we can accomplish when all the women of Protestant churches begin to "possess their possessions," and then go forward under consecrated and intelligent leaders. In the Protestant Church of tomorrow we do not wish the women to stand out as over against the men. We thank God for all they are doing and plan to do. In the different activities to which the Lord has called us, we wish to take our places by their side.

As a loyal Protestant, I believe that the work of the church woman will keep going forward. I am fully aware of the fact that the modern woman is a busy person. At the age of fifty she doesn't put a shawl around her shoulders and sit down in a corner waiting to die. Today a woman of fifty is just in her prime. Her children are grown, and her household routine is lighter than it used to be. She can give more of herself to interests away from home. And nowhere in the world can a Christian woman find a vocation so thrilling as in the work of her own church.

There is a place and a welcome for younger women too. We older ones would let our ideas set like concrete if it were not for the vivacity of those who are younger. Even when there are small toddlers at home, there are ever so many new gadgets to set the young mother free from hard labor part of the time. When it comes to baby-sitting (my daughter says "baby running"), churches are setting up nurseries to care for tots. Young mothers are finding in their church work a way to keep from seeming old before their time.

We also need those who make a living in business. With their love of order and efficiency they can make a contribution of a special kind. The women's work of almost every up-to-date congregation welcomes unmarried businesswomen; in three different churches I took a special interest in them. The abilities and outlook of any one group were different from those of the other two. In each case I discovered one common element, all sorts of know-how and the kind of resourcefulness that every Protestant church needs in its work today. To these business-women I owe a lasting debt.

My friends have helped me to understand the importance of having all the women's work in a congregation organized under a single society. I cannot help noticing that the best answers in the questionnaires come from congregations where all the societies have merged. A typical church in the past had its Ladies' Aid, Women's Auxiliary, Foreign Missionary Society, Home Missionary Society, Pastor's Guild, and all the others. There were "wheels within wheels," but somehow the gears didn't always mesh. Nowadays in almost every denomination the typical forward-looking church has integrated all these groups, and has tried to lead all the women church members into the united work. Perhaps the development of a unified program will prove to be the best thing women have done for the Kingdom. Those of us who have watched this development also believe that the purpose of the united program will be more fully realized in the future. We feel that every church ought to adopt this way of working, rather than looking for some new and fancier way to promote the Kingdom among women. Where it is already under way, the leaders ought to make it operate still more dynamically.

Everywhere societies that have tried the experiment give enthusiastic reports about having all the women work together in one association. Chores previously done by special organizations are now handled by committees or else by circles. One woman writes: "Our principal achievement so far is the gladness with which the women do anything for the church. The efficiency and devotion of our gifted leaders make every public meeting memorable for interest and beauty."

Another slant comes from the South, where the idea of the united church program for women seems to have originated, and where the plan has become well established in many churches. "Our Women's Association is one of the strongest I have ever seen. We have more than seven hundred women engaged in the various circles. Ninety-five per cent of our total budget now goes to missionary projects, whether locally or elsewhere through the denomination.

"In our circles the chief feature is the Bible study program. In each group the devotional leader presents a lesson from the Bible. During the week before the circle gatherings, all the devotional leaders meet with the pastor, who helps them prepare for the lesson. It is a revelation to me how these devoted women have wrestled with and digested the teachings of a difficult book in the Bible."

Another woman writes: "Fellowship is being stimulated throughout our large congregation by the new circle plan. For instance, after morning worship we now have a 'coffee hour' for each of the different districts." The reports go on to show that the united program, with the constituent circles, operates in new and happy ways. When we look beneath the surface we find that these are only new ways of doing old things better. In the circles and in the united work as a whole the women try to encourage Bible-reading and prayer, group worship and private devotions, and enthusiasm for all the work of God's great Kingdom at home and abroad.

Fortunately the plan works as well in a small rural

church at Honeysuckle Valley as in a large congregation on Fifth Avenue. In fact, the work may go even better in a smaller body because the women have fewer distractions. In most cases they simply need assurance about their abilities, proper leadership, and faith in God, who enables his children to work out their own salvation. There is no reason why the workers in any church, however small or remote, cannot take advantage of this plan for better things. In all fairness, I believe that the plan has worked best in a congregation that is neither small nor large, with about five hundred members on the church roll.

Here is word from a rural church that has recently come to life after a long dormant period: " In our women's society we have only thirty-five members, with an average attendance of twenty. We follow the programs as outlined by our denominational Board. We all work together because there are so few of us, and because we are country women." The rest of us can be grateful for such groups. Like other communities of the same sort, this one is filling up with new people. Some of these days that group will need to swarm, so as to have circles that will take care of the newcomers.

For the sake of anyone whose church does not yet have the unified program, let me tell how it works in some of its basic forms. Before anyone broaches the idea of starting a women's association — under whatever name is most common in the denomination — there is need for a good deal of preliminary work. A woman speaker may come from another church of about the same size and in a similar community. She may tell about the way the newer plan was adopted and how it has helped to change the spirit of the women in her church. Before long she stops talking and offers to answer any questions, if she can. Probably

most of these will have to do with small points of organization, rather than searching questions of principle.

In the first meeting the primary question is, How can
we get the women to attend and feel that they want to
take part? As every experienced worker knows, one has to
tickle the curiosity. The only person ready to go ahead,
perhaps, is the minister's wife, but the plan will not move
very far unless she can get someone else to take the lead
in public. Soon she will find that some of the ablest
women would like the work to go as it has been going in
the other church not far away. That persistent question
pops up again: How? How can the change ever come
here? Eventually the time will seem ripe for starting an
organization. Maybe it will take six months, maybe six
years. By having a woman speaker brought in occasionally, distributing denominational literature, talking things
over with friends and, above all, with God, a few women
can prepare the way for a change. If there are already a
number of societies, each representing a minority of the
women in the church, the leaders of these groups must
be won over, though one may stand out to the end as a
" conscientious objector." The groups themselves must be
ready to disband in order to prepare for the merger. This
is like a marriage; nothing ought to be forced.

ERASING THE COLOR LINE

So far we have seen that the Roman Catholics have
something to learn from us about work for laywomen. At
the same time we can learn from them about erasing the
color line. In our city and in others the Roman Catholic
Church is making a determined effort to enlist Negroes
who move into a white community. According to Negro
pastors the effort is meeting with success. In fact, some of

them in our city believe that the Negro may become Roman Catholic, and if he does so, he will give Catholics the balance of power in political affairs.

I am concerned about the attitude any church woman takes toward her new neighbors. Move where she will, she may sooner or later have around her both Negroes and Jews. Shall she treat them as though she is an American and a Christian? In the same place where the apostle says, "There is neither male nor female," he also says, "There is neither Jew nor Greek, there is neither bond nor free." In spirit this appears to mean that as Christians we should treat members of other races as human beings like ourselves. Meanwhile, incoming Negroes say, the one place where they least expect a welcome is in the Protestant Church.

One of our women voicing her problem said: "I like my new Negro neighbors and their children. I have always been in the habit of inviting any new neighbors to attend church with me. But if I took these colored women to church what sort of welcome would they receive?"

Now that the United States Supreme Court has ruled that segregation ought to cease in public schools, some women are asking why it should continue in the Protestant Church. If church buildings are to enjoy freedom from taxation, they should be open to all persons who pay taxes, and to their children.

These are delicate questions, to be sure. They affect women and girls more than they do men and boys. As a former resident in the deep South, and a lover of Southern customs, I have no cheap and easy solution for the problems of race. I do not know what our friends in the South should do. Their situation is considerably different from what we have in the North. But I do not see how any

Protestant woman can close her eyes to the presence of a color line in her home community, nor do I see how she can feel sure of being able to move next time into a community cut off from persons of other races. At the very least, every woman can show kindness to her new neighbors, their children, and their friends. She should have as much concern about the Negro women across the street as about Negro women on the mission field in Africa. In sober truth, charity begins at home.

We might think about the matter of prejudice by considering the other person's point of view. Two Jewish women were riding together on a bus. Sitting directly behind them, I overheard what they said. "You are moving into an awfully nice neighborhood," one of them remarked. "Yes," the other agreed, "I know I am." "Oh," the first woman went on, "there are a few Gentiles, but they don't bother us any."

In almost every church the strategic advantage in meeting newcomers may be taken by the women. If they are willing to receive Negro women as members and friends in the women's association, and invite them to church, the men cannot long refuse to open the doors of the church to all people in the community. During the past twenty years I witnessed a tremendous change in the churches and public schools at Princeton, New Jersey, which previously had a color line. The shift in attitude came about gradually and without any fanfare; and I think it came largely because church women of different races, who believed in God and in one another, came to appreciate and love each other.

The change of attitude came partly through the influence of the late Mrs. T. J. Preston, the former Mrs. Grover Cleveland. Knowing that there was to be a Negro mis-

sionary speaker at a supper in the church, and that some
of the women were not sure how they ought to conduct
themselves, Mrs. Preston came to the meeting, asked if
she might sit at the speaker's table, and through the meal
enjoyed conversation with the Negro gentleman. The
women of the town looked on the former Mrs. Cleveland
as the most gracious of all the wives who have lived in the
White House. They decided they could do no better than
follow her example.

The white population of Princeton trebled in eighteen
years while the community facilities remained static.
School problems became acute. Negro and white children
attended separate schools up to high school age. The building for Negro children was large enough to accommodate
all the junior high children of both races. The problem
was solved by moving the white junior high pupils and
their teachers to the building formerly used exclusively
for Negro children, intermingling the two races in class
work, with the Negro principal in charge. The Negro
grade children and their teachers were intermingled with
the whites in the other building. The plan has been a
success.

At least one Negro girl has joined Old First Church at
Princeton, and another has taught in the Sunday school.
One of the Negro churches has a mixed membership, with
a white man as assistant to the Negro pastor. In the summer of 1954 the three Presbyterian churches, two white
and one Negro, began to meet in union services. Some
years before that the women of the three churches had
joined occasionally in united services. The change is not
complete yet, but it is coming more fully all the time.

While nobody would claim that the women of the
churches brought new patterns of education, alone and

unassisted, it is still true that the entire community felt their influence. These women would not advise churches elsewhere to start a violent crusade, but to begin quietly, in the spirit of prayer, by being kind neighbors with Negro women and children. The Good Samaritan still travels along the rocky road of prejudice.

RELATED READINGS

Anderson, William K., *Protestantism: A Symposium*. Methodist Church Committee on Courses of Study, 1944.

Brauer, Jerald C., *Protestantism in America: A Narrative History*. The Westminster Press, 1953.

Garrison, Winifred E., *A Protestant Manifesto*. Abingdon Press, 1952.

Mays, Benjamin E., *Seeking to Be Christian in Race Relations*. Friendship Press, 1954.

2

AS A LOYAL CHURCH MEMBER

I was glad when they said unto me,
Let us go into the house of the Lord.
— Ps. 122:1.

A CHRISTIAN WOMAN shows her love to Christ by loyalty to the home church. She thinks of her church as the most important place on earth, second only to her home and the dear ones there. Around these two centers her entire life may revolve, and she is glad to have it so. She learns to look on the church as a larger family of God. Someday this woman and her household may have to move. Her husband has been transferred to a distant city, so that in a strange neighborhood they must find another home. They need also to find a church home. In one family that we knew down South the parents were Friends. The husband's work as " trouble man " for cotton mills required him to move frequently. When they came into a community with no Quaker meetinghouse, the entire family attended some other church on the First Day. As soon as they found a place of worship where they felt at home, they adopted that church while in the community. During the years while the children were growing up they lived in a dozen or more communities, and attended that many different churches. Never for a single month did they go without selecting a regular place of worship which they considered their own. The wife and mother really enjoyed her religion, where many other "displaced women " either endure it or else lose it.

FINDING FRIENDS AT CHURCH

When such a woman comes to the church for the first time she ought to receive a welcome, and feel that she is among friends. In these days of shifting populations only the Lord can know how many lonely women there are in any community. One of them recently wrote a magazine article, "I Live in a Suitcase and I Hate It." Time after time, in a strange city or town, she and her husband must put in the week end at a hotel. When they go to church they wish to find God, and to feel at home among his people. Sometimes they are cordially welcomed. More often they run into only a conventional greeting by a church official who knows more about the heating system of the church than about greeting strangers. This kind of greeter shakes hands with a limp " paw " that reminds one of a bunch of shoestrings. While dangling his fingers in your palm he may be looking over your shoulder smiling at someone he knows.

A new woman at church receives less attention than if she were a man, particularly if he is well-groomed and prosperous-looking. She does not want effusive attentions from an officious committee, but she likes to feel the clasp of a friendly hand, and to sense the warmth of heart that lies behind a smile of welcome. An occasional timid woman likes to slip into the church and out again with no one to hinder her coming and going. But the one we are now discussing has had the roots of her family and church life suddenly torn up. Now she wants to feel that she still " belongs " somewhere, and that somebody really cares for her as a human being.

I know by experience. There came a time when I had to give up all the joys of a pastor's wife. After we had

moved away from that church we loved, I felt like a lost
soul. I had experience in several different churches. In a
certain place two or three women gave me a formal nod,
but the majority looked at me as if I might be some new
species of bug! As soon as I presented my membership
certificate and my pedigree I was more than welcome!
Later, for a number of years I went about among women
in another highly favored community. There I discovered
many a lonely woman who longed for the right sort of
friendships to give her a homey feeling when she came
to church. These women did not find fault with the setup,
but, being timid, they waited for us to take the initiative.
If all uprooted families were as earnest as our Quaker
friends in finding a new church home and in making
themselves known to the proper persons, much of our
women's work would be cut in half, and the remaining
half would become an increasing delight.

We Protestant women must learn to be as friendly before and after public worship as we are reverent and at-
tentive in the sanctuary. In such large congregations as
the Broadway Tabernacle in New York and the Euclid
Avenue Baptist Church in Cleveland, some of us have
met such a friendly welcome that we have wished we
lived near enough to " join the happy throng." In other
smaller places of worship, we have found that strangers
can come in and go out for six months without being iden-
tified or made welcome as potential members of the congregation. Perhaps the trouble can be traced to women.

As a church grows older, women tend to form cliques.
As long as they remain friendly, these groups feel free to
go their own ways. Even circles, or other bands of willing workers, become select groups of congenial women,
who feel no need of mingling with strangers whom they

do not know. A congregation composed of such self-centered groups may pride itself on being friendly, because the women have good times whenever they get together. At a girl's college with six or eight hundred students, the same kind of exclusiveness may go on in sororities. The girl with no striking assets feels left out in the cold.

In a congregation that I know well a certain woman never thought of herself as a stranger after she had attended a few church services. She excelled in helping other new members become integrated in the life of the church. A mission-study class was preceded by a luncheon. This woman volunteered to head up the committee for one such meal. She asked two older women familiar with the kitchen to help her, then she drew in a half-dozen newcomers to assist. While peeling potatoes or stringing beans the women all became acquainted. Those who were strangers to everyone at ten o'clock, before it came time to serve the luncheon felt like friends. One of them remarked:

"I must hurry home after class to finish a tablecloth I am crocheting for my daughter."

"What is your pattern?"

"Queen Anne's lace."

"Why, that is my pattern."

"Well," spoke a third, "I'm doing a luncheon set in that pattern myself."

"I think we ought to have a party," said one of the older women. "All of you come to my home next Thursday at three o'clock and bring your crocheting."

Out of this conversation grew a friendly group where everyone felt acquainted with all the rest. While the members crocheted they talked about their children and about the church. One woman was interested in working with the little tots, another in young people's activities, and a third in mission work among the migrants. This crocheting group in no sense formed a clique. Before many months the members all became so engrossed in regular church work that they no longer felt the need of meeting together. Now that they have disbanded for a number of years they still feel grateful for this way of coming to know other women in their church. There is always an extra surge of joy in their hearts when they meet a member of that early group, for those first ties are still strong.

Enjoying Her Church Home

Every normal woman wants a home of her own. She longs for a place she can enjoy with her husband and children. Moreover she wants a church where she can feel equally at home. If she stands ready to do her part as a member she has a right to expect the very best church home that resources can provide. The woman we are thinking about does not envision a great cathedral, where she might feel lost. She wants a homey church large enough to accommodate all the members, and satisfying to the heart of a woman who knows her need of God. Often she may whisper, as she enters the church, " Let me feel Thy presence here."

This woman wants her church to look like a church. She wishes the grounds to be attractive, and always in order. If there is space, she wants to see grass, trees, and other planting, not profuse but restful. Inside she desires to see everything as spotless and inviting as skill and loving hands can make pulpit and pew, because this shows how much we cherish the church. She wants adequate quarters for the spiritual nurture of her children, and attractive places for the women to meet.

More important by far, when a woman comes to her church she has a right to expect an hour of worship that will take her up onto the mountaintop. Music that is worshipful; prayers that come from the heart; Scripture reading and a sermon that interpret life — these open the way to God. During the sacraments, she wants to feel that they bring her household into the very presence of our Lord.

She appreciates a minister who knows her name, and cares about each of her children. She wants to have him in the home, and to hear him pray. If the church is large, and his other parish work is heavy, she is glad to call on him at the church, and there receive counsel about her spiritual needs. She does not want him to become so "busy and troubled" about the needs of the world at large as to forget that he is called first to be the shepherd of the flock to which she belongs. If she had her way, every minister would have to qualify as a good pastor and counselor.

In short, the church woman wants her home church to be a church, and her minister to be its leader.

Nobody plans to start a rebellion. In some congregations the men in charge have permitted spiritual things to be pushed to one side. If I belonged to a church of that sort I should do one of two things. Perhaps I might do both. First I should find other women who felt more or less the same way. I should suggest to each of them that she speak about the matter to the lay church officers she knows, telling them frankly that women in our church want more stress on what we read in the New Testament.

If after a while I found I was making no headway, I

should begin looking about for another church, where I could get spiritual food, light, and uplift for myself and my loved ones, with an opportunity to do a larger share in making the church worthy of my Lord.

Many a dedicated pastor longs for his people, both men and women, to be more faithful in performing their church vows. Three ministers of different denominations, in the same community, sat talking one Sunday evening. Perhaps they were tired after their hardest day in the week. Each was voicing his deep heart longings for his people.

"If I could get every member of my congregation to pledge three hours a week to the church I'd be ready to shout."

"What would you have them do with those three hours?" asked his neighbor.

"I should like one hour for the Bible school, one hour for morning worship, and one hour for the midweek service."

"What about committee meetings and officers' meetings?"

"If I could get this pledge from my members, the extra meetings would follow as a matter of course."

Another spoke: "If I could get all of my people to tithe and give one half of their tithe through the regular church channels, we wouldn't have to be asking for extra money so often. There are other demands on the tithe for good causes which church people should support, but if we could have half of their tithes, I should feel delighted."

The loyal church woman can do much to remove these longings from her pastor's heart by faithfully carrying out the vows she took when she united with the church. Not only will she enjoy her church more; others will too.

ATTENDING THE SERVICES

Sometimes we church women fail to remember that we ought to give even more than we get. When a woman or girl unites with a congregation, she promises in public that she will attend services regularly, and contribute according to her ability. At a different time, perhaps also in the church, she stands "before God and these witnesses," to take her vows of marriage. In each case she promises to give her entire self. Church membership, like marriage, depends on the spirit in which she accepts these ties, and the way she carries them out from week to week.

In answer to my questions one pastor says: "If I could get more of the average church members to take hold and *work,* I'd be a much happier man. So many want to shunt all the responsibilities off onto the pastor and his wife. They could step up church attendance by one half if they exerted themselves a little in friendly calling. Only a few even try to live up to their vows and covenants.

"Another thing that breaks my heart is to see both men and women filing out of church after the Bible class hour. Even among teachers in the Sunday school, women follow their classes out of the church, with never a thought of attending morning worship."

In the right sense of the term churchgoing is a habit. On Sunday morning the thoughts of a Christian woman turn toward the doors of the church. She plans to be there before the hour for vocal worship to begin. During the organ music she can compose her spirit and prepare for what she is about to receive. If she prays for the minister, the choir, and all who worship at the time, she in turn will be ready to receive the blessings the Heavenly Father wishes to bestow. She will have all this and more if she can sit in the pew with her husband and their children. Earth has no fairer picture than this one of a household at prayer together in the church.

The wife and mother in the home has most to do with the formation of this habit. If she marries in the Lord, which is the only way for a Christian woman to marry, she will encourage her husband to attend church regularly. Because of such women in one of our churches, we could count on seventy-five per cent of the members at a regular morning service, fifty per cent at night, and twenty-five per cent at the midweek service. In larger congregations afterward we never again had such a high average of attendance.

Nonattendance also becomes a habit. More people are coming regularly now than in any recent year, according to surveys, but in many churches the average does not yet reach twenty-five per cent. Those who attend at all come regularly. In a congregation with six hundred members, out of a hundred and fifty on a given Sunday, at least a hundred and twenty-five were there a week ago, and will be present next week. Here again, the decision about attending often rests with the wife and mother. Sometimes the business works another way. One Sunday in Kansas City the ten-year-old daughter of a dentist picketed her father's office. On her back she carried a placard: " Unfair to make my daddy work today, because I want him to go to church with me." She got a scolding but she kept on till he quit and took her to church. " A little child shall lead them."

By encouraging her children to attend regularly, the church woman can do much to promote the work of the Kingdom. The habit of churchgoing begins early. Among the men and women who now attend regularly, and are active in church work, the majority formed the habit in childhood. The larger number of ministers, and ministers' wives, and missionaries come from this same group. If any reader questions the statement, let her make a canvass of the church leaders she knows. At what age did they begin to attend church? As soon as they'd entered the beginners' department. " O satisfy us early with thy mercy; that we may rejoice and be glad all our days " (Ps. 90:14).

Fortunately, any of us can change her habits for the better. In my businesswomen's Bible class some of the girls used to protest that attendance there on Sunday morning was enough and ought to take the place of morning worship. Several of them had in their trunks letters of dismissal from other churches. One girl had never been baptized. And yet several of them seemed to think of attendance at Bible class as a substitute for taking part in the public worship. Twenty-five years later, during a recent visit I found that the ones who still reside in the community are regular attendants at church and are active workers in the congregation. While they still teased me about my insistence on their doing " double duty " on the Lord's Day, they agreed that the hour of morning worship in the sanctuary had become increasingly a means of blessing.

SUPPORTING THE CHURCH PROGRAM

Every progressive church has some kind of over-all program. In time each woman who belongs to the congregation ought to find a place for herself. Since the Bible school is the most important part of any church, she may find there an opportunity to teach, or to serve as one of the secretaries. Within the school she can discover a wide variety of opportunities, ranging from wee tots, who need most of all to be loved, up to older women, who also want to be loved, and sometimes humored rather than being left coldly alone. Any woman who has taught children at home should feel ready to volunteer for similar work in the Bible school. If the leaders provide training for work with a certain group of boys and girls, so much the better.

In her enthusiasm for the church school, or some one class, the church woman ought to remember that the school is only a part of the congregation — the most important part, but only a part. In time she may become the president or the teacher of a flourishing Bible class, but she should never let it interfere with the spiritual prosperity of the congregation as a whole.

Another woman may have the ability to sing in the choir. A third may like to work with girl scouts; and a fourth, to visit with shut-in friends. So on through a list of activities as varied as the appeal of Christ to the hearts of women. Without making light of any or all of these beautiful ministries, I would emphasize one other that should enlist every church woman's loyalty and enthusiasm — the cause of missions, which we shall discuss later.

The congregation should afford every woman an attractive opportunity to become well acquainted with the entire enterprise of her denomination, as it stands committed to winning the world to Christ. The leaders of our men's work often tell each other that missions is the lifeblood of Christianity. They might also add that the lifeblood comes from the heart, and that, in almost every church, women are the very heart of missionary enthusiasm, prayers, and programs.

All the women of the home church at work for the winning of the world to Christ, especially the women and the

girls, for no nation can rise above the level of its women
— what a " vision splendid "!

RELATED READINGS

Blackwood, Andrew W., *Pastoral Work*. The Westminster
Press, 1945.

Cain, H. P., *The Church Ministering to Rural Life*. The
Church of the United Brethren in Christ, 1945.

Corson, Fred P., *Your Church and You*. John C. Winston
Company, 1951.

Harrell, Costen J., *The Local Church in Methodism*. Abingdon Press, 1952.

Harrington, Janette T., *Looking at the City*. Friendship Press,
1954.

Hendricks, Garlans A., *Biography of a Country Church*. The
Broadman Press, 1950.

Hewitt, Arthur W., *God's Back Pasture*. Willet, Clark & Company, 1941.

Shippey, Frederick A., *Church Work in the City*. Abingdon
Press, 1952.

3

AS AN ACTIVE CHURCH WORKER

As we have many members in one body,
and all members have not the same office:
so we, being many, are one body in Christ,
and every one members one of another.
— Rom. 12:4, 5.

IN THE QUESTIONNAIRE I asked each minister, "How do you find new workers among women?" One pastor replies facetiously, "We don't!" Another writes, "They come to the top like cream." A third reports, "The women themselves keep things shuffled." Still another replies, "Pray, then ask." All these men agree that there should be a work for every woman, and every woman should be at work. There is nothing about most church activity that calls for gifts and graces beyond the reach of any woman in the church. The larger the church, the greater is the variety of work to be done. The smaller the body, the more need there is for urging every woman to take part.

The very idea of a body means that every member ought to receive and give. In a church body the woman member ought to receive spiritual food, fresh air, and an opportunity to exercise her spiritual muscles. Otherwise she may begin to suffer from fatty degeneration of the soul. Not including shut-in saints, the most spiritual women of any church are not only diligent in attending church and enjoying worship; they are equally active in showing the meaning of their creed by the beauty of daily living, "always abounding in the work of the Lord."

Usually women can control their time better than men,

42

many of whom work for others, and by the clock. Then too most women are more socially minded. They can see the importance of what some men think of as little things, like calling on the sick and taking flowers to shut-ins. To a woman who loves the Lord and his Church, nothing in the way of service seems little or meaningless. If any reader will make a list of all the varied activities that appear on succeeding pages, she will find an astonishing array, much of it involving detail and requiring patience, tact, and a winning smile, with what Mrs. Rorer used to call " a glass roller and a magic hand."

SERVING ON A COMMITTEE

Every woman who shows a willingness to work eventually finds herself on a committee. If she does her part, she need never again feel that she has been given nothing to do in the church. Women's work is organized largely in the way of committees, some of them active and others not. A woman should accept appointment on only one committee at a time. If she has no special concern about the business in hand, she might well study it all the more, until she becomes an enthusiast. By well-aimed questions she can learn from former committee members what has been done and what needs to be done.

She can also write to the denominational headquarters. There she can get literature about the work of her committee — literature well written and often free for the asking. All that the people at headquarters can do is to help set up ideals, fix goals, and make practical suggestions about ways and means for the local society. Afterward the committee member can begin to dream and pray and plan about applying these theories to her particular situation.

One thing she ought to remember from the first. No matter how full of ideas she may be, a committee member should never try to take the place of the chairman. Someday the member herself will be a chairman, let us hope. Then she will wish her committee members to observe the Golden Rule, namely, Be a good follower, and honor your leader. Also cheer the team, instead of sitting in the seat of the scornful or on the mourners' bench. As chairman someday she will be thankful for the member who always attends committee meetings, understands everything that comes up, and is ready to help in anything the chairman asks or suggests.

In any businesslike society most of the detail work is done by committees. Meeting privately, a small group of women take up each opportunity or problem, and deal with it thoughtfully. Sooner or later they come to what Quakers call "the sense of the meeting." Next the report goes before the entire executive board, and, if necessary, is presented to the society as a whole. After the committees have reported briefly, the larger group can turn to something inspirational. Meanwhile the work advances. If all committee work among our women's societies functioned this way, an organization could double its usefulness in a single year. The idea is to keep in the committee room the details that do not interest or concern the larger group.

The effectiveness of committee work depends largely on the chairman, who should have a knack for finding and using other workers. Here is Mrs. Willing, goodhearted, eager, but tactless, who complains: "Why do they put Mrs. Z on that committee as chairman? She never has gone to college. Here I am a graduate of Radcliffe, and they never ask *me* to serve as chairman of anything!"

Both statements were true. On the other hand the woman who has never gone to Bryn Mawr or Wellesley may develop an inferiority complex. So it seems that the one least qualified to lead wants to stand in the limelight, while the one who has all the necessary grace may shrink from taking the lead.

College training has its place. It helps to prepare many women for leadership in the church and in larger circles. But no college diploma can guarantee the presence of charm and tact, and ability to solve problems. Mrs. Z had all these marks of leadership, and soon won the love and respect of others as a leader.

The Radcliffe graduate was equally kindhearted and still more eager to serve. She was specially concerned about the work of a certain benevolent society, which was loosely organized, and held only one meeting a year. Since no one else seemed able to accept the office, Mrs. Willing was invited to act as convener. She gladly accepted, and asked to have the gathering in her beautiful and spacious home. After the meeting had started, haphazardly, late-comers rang the doorbell. Dropping everything else, the college graduate rushed to the door, welcomed the new-comers effusively, showed them where to put their wraps, and hunted up extra chairs. Evidently she had not been taught at school how to plan for a meeting and how to get others to do everything but preside. And yet this mistress of confusion wondered why women preferred the leadership of a noncollege woman who planned everything as carefully as for a formal evening reception with the same number of invited guests.

Another woman without tact kept insisting that she ought to have a larger opportunity to serve. In a meeting of the committee to which she had been appointed, the chairman unwisely asked to have someone volunteer for a certain mission. Of course Mrs. Eager Beaver spoke out, " I will go." She was to visit a nominee in the name of the committee to prevail on this woman to accept an appointment. In the press of other duties, for she had many irons in the fire, Mrs. Eager Beaver forgot what the committee wished this friend to do. But that little detail was of minor importance!

As soon as she entered the door she blurted out breathlessly: " The women want you to do something in the missionary society. I've forgotten just what it is, but it isn't anything very important." Fortunately the nominee had a sense of humor. Through more reliable channels she later found out what it was that the committee wanted her to do, and she accepted the appointment and did her work with distinction. Incidentally she made her own assignments on her committee and did not ask for volunteers. Like autumn apples in an orchard, the best fruit is always hand picked.

Working on a Nominating Committee

In the questionnaire to laywomen, I asked, " How do you keep your society from getting into ruts? " The ones who had no such difficulties reported using the rotary system, and " interest cards " with new women members. When anyone joins the church or the association she is asked to fill out a card showing her past experience as a church woman, and her interests as a potential worker. These cards are available to the nominating committee. If the committee is wide awake, the new woman may soon be asked to serve in a minor capacity, though she need never be told that it is " unimportant."

The effectiveness of the plan, and of the work in general, depends for the most part on members of the nominating committee. These women have an untold opportunity for usefulness. If they act unwisely, or thoughtlessly, they may do more harm than good. It is no light matter to guide a society in selecting its officers for the next two years. Experience has shown that this is a satisfactory working period, and so we shall think in terms of two years as the limit.

The rotary system was born out of sad experience. In older days, when the women in office had been faithful and effective leaders they would continue year after year, as if according to some law of the Medes and Persians. In most cases the women grew less efficient as the beaten track deepened into a rut. Even when the officers retained all their ability, the plan failed to develop other leaders. Then, too, the society became known as " the old women's group." As these senior leaders died off, the number of workers dwindled.

Today, in every live association, all this has changed. If the rotary system really rotates, it excuses every officer after she has served two years, and then brings in another. At the beginning of a united work, it is best to have half of the newly elected officers serve for only one year. Then there need be no complete change of personnel in any one year. As a consequence, the work of the executive board can go forward immediately after the installation of new officers. In a very successful body, experience shows the need of new blood.

To all these rules about rotation I suggest that there be a single exception. Other officers come and go, but the treasurer ought to hold her office as long as she excels. There need be no written rule, for occasionally it may be necessary to excuse even a treasurer from her arduous labors, which she may have bungled. But when a society once lays hands on a treasurer who knows how to report hilarious giving, she will be worth her weight in rubies. In two successive societies I have known such women, who could secure both money and admiration from all the women of the society, and from some of the men too. One such treasurer adds a dash of humor as she reads her report, so that the women pay close attention to what she says. For example, " The offering last month was $97.50 and one cough drop! "

The number of women on a nominating committee should vary according to the size of the organization. In a large society there may be seven, or even nine; in a smaller group, only three, of course beginning with the chairman. In some societies these women are appointed each year a few months before the annual meeting for election of officers. In other groups the committee serves for two years, just as the officers do. Then if there is an unexpected vacancy the standing committee can bring in a nomination without delay.

The president of the association may select the chairman and the members of this committee, after asking for the approval of the executive board. Every member, especially the chairman, ought to be familiar with the over-all program of the church. They ought also to know the members. For this reason the chairman of the membership committee may well serve here, ex officio, since her work leads her to know the women of the church more or less intimately.

After the nominating committee has been selected, the chairman ought to call a meeting soon. This meeting should begin with prayer for the guidance of the Holy Spirit. The members also should agree that any discussion of a proposed nominee be held in confidence, and that no information be given out until the final nominations are ready to be presented to the society. Strange as the fact may seem to the menfolk, we women *can* keep a secret. If a woman cannot, she ought to be on the publicity committee and be excused from helping to make nominations. The chairman of the nominating committee ought to present the slate of officers when the time has come to do so. When a woman is appointed on a committee she does not automatically become " speaker of the house."

ENLISTING NEW LEADERS

Especially in churches of long standing the tendency is to keep the reins of government in the hands of older women. Surely no society ought to dispense with the wisdom of women who long have borne the burdens of the work. They know the local traditions, and they can keep things on an even keel. But sometimes the younger woman, with her new interest and energy, can do more in the way of onward motion. If the older ones can keep the younger women from making rash adventures, the younger ones can keep the mothers in Israel from growing stale. It is a safe rule: " Mix the older ones with the younger ones. When in doubt, give the preference to the young."

First of all, the committee should decide on the nominee for president. If she is willing to serve, they may ask her, in confidence, about some of the other nominees. Without pulling any wires, the committee may feel responsible for nominating someone who will accept. In one of our churches the committee had decided on a Mrs. A, who had no church background, and had been a professing Christian for only a few years. When the committee could not persuade her to accept the nomination, the chairman appealed to the pastor and his wife. For a week the two of us gave to this matter more attention and prayer than to anything else. We have felt ever since that the choice was providential. Neither of us would ever have thought of suggesting Mrs. A for that office. The idea came from a committee member.

In another congregation the chairman said to her committee, " Of all the women we have discussed, Mrs. Able would be my first choice." " She would be wonderful," said another, " but she is in so many outside things. Do you suppose she could be persuaded to accept? " " There is one way to find out. We can ask her." " You are the chairman. You ask her. Mrs. Able is a woman of prayer. She has tact and charm and ability and poise. She is always well groomed. She knows how to preside. In fact, she seems to have everything, and she would be a credit to us wherever she appeared."

The chairman agreed about all of this, and consented to extend the invitation at once. Instead of telephoning, or writing a letter, she went in person. She found Mrs. Able surprised, pleased, feeling honored, but still hesitant. " You know I have my family duties. I am on the P.T.A. board, the Y.W.C.A. council, the Red Cross committee, and I work with the civic group. I don't see how I can find time to do any more." The chairman had thought about these matters and had her answers ready.

"My dear, that is just the reason why all the committee want you for this very important post. We know about your work in these other excellent organizations, but still we all feel that with you as a Christian woman Christ and his church ought to come first. If you feel obliged to give up some of your present work, other women can take it up because you have shown them how. We have no one else in sight for the leadership of the women's work in our church. Do not give me your decision now. Pray about it and talk it over with your husband and children. See if they do not want you to put the church first. Let me know when you decide to say yes."

Two days later the committee rejoiced when Mrs. Able telephoned that she felt honored to accept their invitation. They then went on to complete the list of nominees. In due time they were elected and installed, to begin the very best year in the history of the women's work in that church. Had they not sought and followed the guidance of the Holy Spirit?

A missionary from Brazil told me how this idea worked among the women in the station where she served. As in apostolic times they came together to select leaders. There had been no pre-election campaign for any one person. They left all of that to the Lord. "Thou, Lord, who knowest the hearts of all, show us which of these [women] thou hast chosen." (See Acts 1:24.) Then they voted, and, amazingly, the vote was almost always unanimous. If the woman whom they chose did not feel worthy to accept, or capable of serving, the friends would say to her: "You have no choice but to serve. You were elected by the Holy Spirit." The missionary said that such experiences had occurred in various churches thereabouts, so that they came to look on the women's work as under the guidance of the Spirit. How different from the scene that follows!

BUNGLING THE LORD'S BUSINESS

"Mrs. A, will you serve as chairman of the nominating committee?"

" Glad to, then I won't have to take an office." (Hilarious mirth!)

" We need two other members. Will you choose them? "

" Sure. There's Mrs. B and Mrs. C, both swell girls! " (More laughter.)

The days roll into weeks. At last Mrs. A corrals the other two " swell girls " after church one morning and says: " Say, we ought to have a meeting. We'll have to report next Tuesday." Then Mrs. C has a bright idea:

" Why don't we get off in a corner and have a meeting now? Let's make it snappy because I have to get home and start dinner."

So they find a corner. Mrs. B reports that if nobody else will take the job, one of her friends has come and volunteered to serve.

" O.K.," says the happy chairman. " Who is this glad sister? " " Mrs. Unable," was the reply.

" Swell! She's on the ball. She has loads of time, and drives a Cadillac. What are we waiting for? Put her down for president, and she can choose the other officers."

" Do you suppose she knows anything about presiding? Can she lead in prayer out loud? " said Mrs. B timidly.

" Oh, I don't know," said the chairman. " If she doesn't she can learn. There's really nothing to it. So let's quit and get out of here. Everything O.K.? "

The next Tuesday the report of the committee was received. Mrs. Unable and her appointees were elected. Not knowing anything about parliamentary law, and never having presided over a meeting, she came to her first one full of assurance. Perhaps because of unusual care in preening, she was late in arriving. Still she made an effective entrance. " Solomon in all his glory " was not arrayed like Mrs. Unable. With a picture hat and an elab-

orate gown that would have graced a reception for the
governor, she had slung over her shoulder a costly fur
scarf. She sailed down the middle aisle to the front row
of seats, looked at the clock on the wall, then at her
diamond-studded wrist watch. Shaking the watch, she
said in a stage whisper,

"Guess it must uv stopped."

Now that her hour of triumph had come, the would-be
leader felt a sense of panic. She started for the platform,
but stubbed her toe on the top step, and almost catapulted
into the waiting chair. First she righted herself and carefully draped her fur scarf over the back of another chair,
so that everybody could see it. Next she scrambled
through the litter on the desk for a hymnal, which was not
there. A woman down front handed her one. Then the
leader spoke out, perhaps thinking her first words ought
to be memorable.

"Does anyone have a song to suggest?" Gladly she
accepted the first suggestion, and called for the "first and
last verses," only to find that no one was ready to play
the piano.

And so the meeting went along, from bad to worse.
There was no plan, no order, no sense of being there to
carry forward the business of the King. Nothing but confusion, frustration, and lost opportunity. Why? Because
somebody had blundered in choosing the chairman of the
nominating committee.

If anyone thinks these pictures are overdrawn, I can
assure her that I am reporting what I have seen, with
only enough changes in detail to hide from others the
identity of the victims. Really both Mrs. Willing and
Mrs. Eager Beaver were goodhearted women. They were
merely trying to grace a chair for which they had had no

training or knowledge. For a contrasting picture, look at
the following, which also comes from real life.

DIGNIFYING THE KING'S BUSINESS

In St. Paul, Minnesota, a nominating committee followed a plan that seems to me unique. The committee
met and, after much prayer, selected a woman for each
office. Then the committee sent out invitations for tea,
with the members of the committee as hostesses. The
invitations went to all the present officers and the nominees, but with no hint about the purpose of the gathering, which was held in a private home. After a happy time
of social enjoyment the chairman of the committee called
the women to order and delivered what she called a
" charge."

"Members of the Women's Association, your nominating committee's work has often been a real ' headache.'
They telephoned to various women and asked them to
accept certain offices. Almost invariably the committee
members received refusals and excuses. The members
came to dislike their job immensely. They said they felt
more like beggars than anything else.

"Our new plan calls for the selection of persons to be
nominated under two basic principles: First, who is the
most capable woman for this particular office? Secondly,
does she truly love Christ and his Church? We feel sure
that when once a woman is selected who fulfills these
two requirements there will be no refusal, and no excuses.
In our homes we often do things that we do not like. We
never think of making excuses, but simply go ahead and
do what needs to be done. So we ought to do the same
in our relationship with Christ. If we love him we do not

hesitate to ask questions about the services that he calls us to perform.

"You women gathered here as guests of the committee are being 'called' to offices in our women's organization. You have been selected with great care, only after much prayer for guidance. We feel confident that our prayers have been answered, and that each of you is the best possible person for the office. We have no second choices.

"I shall now read the title of each office and the name of the woman selected for that office. After the list has been read I shall ask each of you to rise to give your answer. We pray that you will answer in the affirmative, and that before we leave today we may have our nominations complete."

The president of the group reports that this procedure worked beautifully. If it differs from the plan I have outlined above, all the better. The Holy Spirit does not guide every group to follow the same pattern. But he always guides, if we put ourselves in his hands and if we wish to do his will.

Related Readings

Cavert, Inez M., *Women in American Church Life*. Friendship Press, 1954.

Kirk, Jane, "Women's Place in the Church," in the *Christian Herald*, issued monthly.

Mathews, Winifred, *Dauntless Women*. Friendship Press, 1954.

Peare, Catherine O., *Mary McLeod Bethune*. Vanguard Press, Inc., 1951.

Wyker, Mossie A., *Church Women in the Scheme of Things*. Bethany Press, 1953.

4

AS A REGULAR CHURCH OFFICER

Let me introduce our sister Phoebe, a
deaconess of the church at Cenchreae; receive her in the Lord. . . . She has been a
help . . . to many people, including myself.
— Rom. 16:1, 2 (Moffatt).

S HOULD WOMEN SERVE on the regular boards of the congregation, and of the Church at large? I asked laywomen, "Do you think the women should have a larger
part in the work of the local church?" The replies cover
such a wide field that they are difficult to summarize.
Those who merely say *yes* or *no* are exactly fifty-fifty.
Others reply: "Not necessarily." "We believe that if the
women had a larger share the men would lose their interest." Evidently the women keep on working even if they
do not hold so many prominent offices as the men. "We
could furnish plenty of capable women if they were
needed, but the men seem to be doing a good job." "We
have all we can do now." "We are already equally represented." In other words, don't upset something that is
functioning satisfactorily.

SERVING ON BOARDS WITH MEN

One minister writes that his entire board of deacons is
composed of women, and they are his "right arm in a host
of details." Here it seems that the men handle the big
things, and do them well. Several pastors report that half
their deacons are women. In other churches the women

serve on the board of trustees, and in some places they act as elders or other spiritual leaders of the flock. In some branches of Protestantism women can of course become fully ordained ministers and serve as pastors of churches, but we do not need to consider that matter now. Up to the present time few women have chosen to become ministers.

The majority of the pastors seem to be willing for the women to be on the "men's boards," but some laymen resent the presence of "skirts" at their meetings. This applies especially to the men who handle the money and other business affairs. Their meetings are often rather informal and they do not want anyone around to "cramp their style." In most cases they do not welcome even the pastor unless he leaves soon after the opening prayer. As for women members, the men say: "Why can't a group of women get together without letting the whole church know what has been done at the trustees' meeting the night before? Often we talk about tentative plans which are not yet ready for general publicity." The pastor who wrote this "gripe," to use his own word, ought to remember that male members of such boards have been known to let secrets slip out prematurely. The habit of keeping one's mouth shut about a secret matter, and of talking freely about confidential things, has never yet been confined to either sex. Both men and women need to learn how to control the tongue.

I asked the ministers to state their chief difficulties in dealing with women workers. The replies came from pastors who rely largely on women helpers, including those elected to boards composed chiefly of men. These frank revelations ought to have a sobering effect on those of us who serve in any capacity. We need to recall Bobby

Burns's song with a queer name, " To a Louse ":

> " Oh wad some power the giftie gie us
> To see oursels as others see us!
> It wad frae monie a blunder free us,
> An' foolish notion."

Here is part of what the ministers reveal about women: " Sometimes, though seldom, picayune." " They want the limelight." " Jealousy." " Smallness in trivial matters." " Occasional intramural bickerings." " Slowness in arriving at decisions." " Pettiness." " The great mission of the Church should subordinate all the difficulties. Too often the women let the difficulties subordinate the great mission of the Church." " Chief difficulty is to keep their sights high."

" Women are a little more inclined to be childish than men." (We prefer to say " childlike," since our Lord often told his followers to become " like little children.") " Occasional personality conflicts." " Not all Christians have grown enough in spiritual matters as to be free from self-will in service." We should feel grateful for all these comments, and in reply say: " Guilty, dear brethren. Pray for us." I especially like the candor of the minister who confesses that his chief failing lies in " not keeping warm-hearted, understanding, and tactful on my part." If more pastors adopted a similar attitude they would have fewer headaches in their work with women.

Every one of us could make a " retort courteous." But let's face it. All of us have met women who displayed some of these objectionable traits. So let us search our own hearts in the light of these reports from ministers, every one of whom I know to be honest, high-minded, and consecrated.

PREPARING FOR ACTIVE SERVICE

The trend at present is toward larger activity by women on the boards where men used to have a monopoly. Especially during the war years women and girls showed their ability to work shoulder to shoulder with men in what we used to consider men's work. Of course the women needed to be trained, but they learned quickly. When each of our world wars ended it left a large number of women working side by side with men. In many of the more progressive churches today the same holds true. Sometimes we women take up the new duties without any preliminary training. What can a woman do to prepare for service on a " men's board "?

Begin by sending to headquarters for denominational literature about the board on which you are to serve. Then digest this literature until you can stand a self-imposed examination. You will find in it both the purpose of the board and your own duties. As for the meetings of the " men's board," for the first few times maintain a discreet silence. If you are asked for an opinion, speak up, but briefly, and not too decidedly. Even male members, when elected to serve on a board, if they are smart, get accustomed to the run of things before they begin to take an active part. So gently " break " the men into glad acceptance of your presence among them.

But keep on being a woman, with all of your charm and reserve. Too often when a woman goes into politics she tries to ape men, by developing a raucous voice, taking long strides, and seeming to be hail-fellow-well-met. All that may be acceptable among some of the men in ward politics, but let us assume that the men on church boards are all Christian gentlemen. With them the age of chivalry is not dead, not even dying. They want a woman to be every inch a woman. Down in their hearts they shy away from a mannish woman, just as we do from a womanish man.

In such meetings be courteous and considerate. Know the rules of the game, and then play it fairly and squarely. Do not expect men to defer to your judgment just because you are a woman. Assume equality with the men, but not superiority. If a matter of conscience arises, such as the use of the church for questionable purposes, stand your ground, but do it pleasantly. If you do not get your way all at once, the skies will not fall. In dealing with men remember that some of them like to argue. If you state a matter strongly and begin to make a case, these " fellows " will at once find a dozen reasons why you are wrong. In such situations follow the example of Maggie in Sir James M. Barrie's delicious little drama *What Every Woman Knows.* The author shows that she can deal with her man without letting him know that he is being led.

Certain pastors report that women, when elected to church boards, soon become much better informed than the men. Before long the women discover that the groups do not always live up to the ideals in the denominational literature. Instead of demanding immediate and drastic reforms, they can bide their time, and work indirectly. The results are so pleasing that one pastor writes:

" It seems to me a fallacy to have men and women separated in church work. We are moving more and more toward having them teamed together in the administration of all our affairs. Both the women and the men like it, and so does the minister. They serve on the same committees, perform much the same tasks, and enjoy being with each other. They keep saying, not, ' The women have done this and the men have done that,' but rather, 'We all have done this and that, working together.'"

HOPING FOR A BETTER PLAN

In certain forward-going churches we find an official board which co-ordinates and unifies all the work of the congregation. On such a board both men and women serve as representatives of all important societies and activities in the congregation, including the young people. These leaders look at the work of the congregation as a whole, and make plans for it, so that no one organization or department will overshadow another.

Any such plan leaves room for all the activities the community needs, and still goes far to show that no part of the church will function with little reference to the other parts. Just as "the eye cannot say unto the hand, I have no need of thee," so the men's class cannot tell the women's missionary society, or vice versa, "We have nothing to do with you." In these days when we keep talking about more co-operation and unity among the diverse parts of Protestantism we ought to begin by having co-operation and unity among the organizations in a given church. Whenever that day comes, women will feel at last that they have an equal opportunity to do their full share in promoting the Kingdom.

Under the right sort of trained ministerial leadership this way of working operates equally well in a small wayside chapel and in a large metropolitan congregation. Since most of our women work in churches of average size, we can think most about such fields. The plan is so elastic that it permits expansion of committees to meet new needs as they become apparent and to slough off old ways when they seem to be outmoded. A church need not try to serve a changing population with methods inherited from day before yesterday. For our part in a working Church today and tomorrow we women should be ready to act intelligently.

SERVING AS A DISTRICT LEADER

One of the most satisfactory developments in church work is that of dividing the parish into geographical districts. The ways of doing so must be adapted to the work of the denomination, the type of community, and the size of the working force. The key idea is to have one or two persons in each geographical area. They become responsible for keeping in touch with all the members, the adherents, and the prospective members, who live in that district. Just as in the early days of the British Empire the queen could get in touch with every subject in less than twenty-four hours, so can the church secretary reach all the members within any one day. Naturally she does not trouble them about trivial things.

Some such plan seems imperative today because of shifting population. Statisticians tell us that during the war years 40 per cent of our people moved from one locality to another, and that in normal times 18 per cent of our people change residence every year. Church statisticians also estimate that among Protestants who move from one community to another 50 per cent are lost to the Church. Large numbers of "nonresident members" become church tramps. Eventually they lose their concern about Christ and the Church, just at the time when their lonely hearts most need what the Church has to give.

Even with those who own their own homes and remain in the community there is need of a person or persons to keep them in touch with the church. Somebody ought to report in case of illness or accident, the birth of a baby, or the return of a loved son from the armed services. Women should plan to do this part of the work as well as party workers do with their "block system"! In a city organized this way the political party leader can get in touch with any person in a given block.

A large church we know has 50 men who serve that many districts; they could do the work better if there were also 50 women. Every district leader is responsible for about 50 church members, and for persons who may move into the district without having a church home. The district leader keeps in touch with the members, and they with the leader. When a new family moves into a district, the immediate neighbors notify him. Together the workers decide what needs to be done. They do not trouble the pastor or the church office about trifles; neither do they fail to report immediately anything important.

Strange as it may seem, more than one large church keeps in closer touch with its members, and with newcomers in the community, than do the smaller churches from which the newcomers moved. The larger the church, and the more shifting its constituency, the more the need of an up-to-the-minute district system, with both a man and a woman as the official representatives of the church in every geographical area that it serves. In their replies the pastors report that a man and a woman serve best as leaders if they come from different homes. However, where circumstances make it necessary, a husband and wife can render effective service, especially if the calls must be made at night. Each visitor depends on person-to-person contacts, and not on the telephone or the mail carrier.

In one rural church the women's Bible class takes charge

of this work. The members in each district go two by two and call at every home in the community, whether or not the people belong to the church. To nonmembers the visitors extend a hearty welcome to the community and a cordial invitation to the church and the Bible class. They also notify the pastor about the newcomers, and their past affiliations, if any. Since this is a community church, the callers feel free to invite people of different faiths. This is real missionary work. Twenty-five years ago everybody thought of this church building as an empty shell and the church as dying. Now the work is going forward, among the women in particular.

Pastor after pastor reports that women make ideal district leaders. They visit the sick and shut-in members, reporting serious illness or any emergency. As for newcomers, what woman can restrain her curiosity when she sees the moving van unloading next door, or halfway down the block? If she is a district leader, she is a "natural" to go at once to the new family and ask if she can help. She may not go into the house for a day or two, but she can offer the use of her telephone, and give up-to-date information about where to secure supplies. Such neighborly attentions by a church leader mean twice as much the first day or week as if one waited a month or two.

Recently we have made two moves, one of which left us cold so far as neighbors were concerned. In the second move the next-door neighbor came over at once and offered the use of her telephone, or anything else that we needed. During that first week after the moving I did not have to think once about the evening meal. Kind friends supplied our needs there. Fortunately we did not need an introduction to a church, but if we had been like most newcomers we should have felt all at sea. As in transplanting shrubbery, the life and growth in strange soil may depend on whether or not there is rain. In the case of a family moving to a strange community, the " rain " comes best through Christian kindness on the part of church people who live nearby.

I am not suggesting that the district leader rush out and invite the new family for dinner, but she can take a bouquet of flowers from her garden, a few cookies, or some small token of kindness. When our friends, the Einsteins, moved into their own home, they came to us for cleaning cloths! They also told us they had food, but as yet had not unpacked cutlery or dishes. Their gratitude was touching when I took down the needed articles with a pitcher of hot soup. In dealing with new neighbors it is not so much the deed itself as the timeliness of it, and the kindness that prompts it.

Without seeming " nosy " a district leader can learn about the church connections of the new family. If they belong to her branch of the Church, or if there is no church of their denomination, she invites them to attend with her. Perhaps she may offer to take them in the family car. Especially for the younger members of the family, she extends an invitation to the church school, and, if agreeable, has some of the young people stop by. She reports the pertinent facts to the church office.

If the new family belong to another branch of the Church the leader tells them where to find the nearest church of their choice. Then she reports the facts to the pastor concerned. When a family of Episcopalians moved in across the street from us, we called and welcomed them as neighbors and then notified the nearest rector, who called the next day. The family united with his church. In all these neighborly contacts a leader must be careful not to "steal sheep." Every church and pastor ought to follow the Golden Rule.

A district captain does not try to do all this work herself. In visiting among her 50 members, more or less, she enlists each woman as a sort of block worker, to extend a hand of welcome to a new family near her home. If two families show the strangers Christian kindness, that will be two more than with most "displaced persons" these days. Because of timidity, or cowardice, most church women tend to do nothing, and let the pastor find these potential members six months after the introduction ought to have come from a neighbor.

In due time the leader arranges a tea for the women members of her district. She also invites others who have no church home. She may plan for an evening gathering, with both men and women, either at the church or in some home. There they can all meet the pastor and his wife, and get to know each other. We who are established and have many social engagements and opportunities forget that such events rarely come into the lives of some church members. Too many people move into a new community where all the doors seem to be shut.

In more than one church that we have known, my husband and I have wondered why the officers do not plan for some such intensive cultivation in the community surrounding the church. Time and again we have met people in need of a church home who had never been discovered by the people living across the street, or by those who sit in the same pew during morning service. On the other hand, we have found more than a few churches so well districted and manned, or rather "womaned," that no family can move into the community, and no stranger can visit the church, without receiving a Christian welcome and sensing the opportunity to make this a church home.

Some reader may protest, "That is all very well in a large church, but what can we do with our relatively small numbers?" Well, don't cultivate an inferiority complex. The keenest students of church management tell us that every time you double the size of an average church you quadruple the difficulty of organizing workers so that there will be no overlapping of effort and no overlooking of persons in need. If the churches that do the most intensive work through district leaders are not small and weak bodies, one reason may be that the block system brings in new families, and makes them feel so much at home that they become active members of their new church.

If you have an opportunity to become a church officer, you ought to accept. From the inside, you can pray and work and hope for the coming of the time when your church will plan its methods so as to care for all the spiritual needs of every person for whom the congregation is responsible. Lift up your heart — "Who knoweth whether thou art come to the kingdom for such a time as this?" (Esth. 4:14).

5

AS A MISSIONARY PROMOTER

Seek ye first the kingdom of God, and his righteousness;
and all these things shall be added unto you.
— Matt. 6:33.

WHAT DO YOU CONSIDER the principal achievements
of your women's organizations?" This question
brought enthusiastic replies from nearly all the pastors
who reported. Almost without exception they put at the
head of the list the women's missionary activities. All the
ministers are careful to state that this is only one of
the many fine contributions made by women. Some replies
refer to the change from the olden days in our country,
when women were supposed to "keep silent" in the worship and work of the church. In order to appreciate how
far such work for women has advanced, let us look back
at the beginnings here in the United States.

LOOKING AT THE BEGINNINGS

The records do not show clearly with whom missionary
work among women began. After the Revolutionary War
a number of groups banded themselves together to help
the men to raise money for missionary work at home and
abroad. Some of the earliest groups were among the
Quakers. The first definite record seems to be that of the
Female Cent Society, formed by the Baptist women of
Boston in 1800. The organized missionary work of the
Congregational women seems to have begun in 1801; of
Presbyterian women, in 1803; of the Dutch Reformed, in

1815; and of the Methodist, in 1819. Others may have been equally early.

"The significant thing, however, is not which denomination originated the idea of 'female societies,' or when or where. It is that in spite of the terrific handicaps they faced, church women had the temerity to form societies in days when such a movement was not looked upon with favor by the brethren — not even by the male members of their own families, to say nothing of the pastors and elders." (From *Daughters of Dorcas,* by Florence Hayes.)

In the beginning the groups were small, and few in number, but the enthusiasm was great. Like their menfolk in blazing new trails, our foremothers had to make their own precedents and develop their own customs. Where else in history could they find anything like a pattern for laywomen to follow in promoting missionary work more and more their own? They were guided largely by prayer, and in turn they felt assured of the leading of the Holy Spirit. Today in almost every church and denomination we can do no better than to wear their mantle of missionary service, with a double portion of their loyalty to Christ and missions. A double portion here means the eldest daughter's share in the family estate, so that she can render twice as much service as any of her sisters.

These early wives and mothers, with their large families and without any of our electrical aids to housework, must have been too busy to leave complete records. The records that remain provide some of the most fascinating reading matter I have ever found. At Princeton the early accounts report that one woman read aloud while others prepared boxes for " the heathen," likewise sewing underwear and shirts, with " false collars " and " false bosoms " for " poor but pious students at the theological seminary."

All the while, as everywhere else, the meetings were begun, continued, and ended in the spirit of Bible-reading
and fervent prayer for the unsaved at home and to the
ends of the earth.

Those early women labeled themselves with names as
odd and even lugubrious as some of their old-time bon-
nets and shawls. Think of the " Female Benevolent Society," the " Female Praying Society," the " Female Cent
Society," and the " Female Society for the Support of a
Female School in India." Surely these founding mothers
wished everyone to know that they were females and not
ashamed of their womanhood. They must have felt that
in missions as in the home it is not good that woman
should be alone. So the constitution of one such " female "
group contains this clause:

" The society shall have a patron who shall be some respectable gentleman, to be chosen by the society at the
annual meeting." The responsibility for finding this " respectable gentleman " lay with the president and the secretary. Once secured, according to the record, " he will
come to open our meetings with Scripture and prayers."
One divine, evidently " respectable," insisted that some
man ought always to be present at every missionary meeting of the women, because " if left to themselves, there is
no telling what they might pray for."

In one of the best-known denominations an early record
tells of the following action by the chief assembly, of
course composed of men: " A meeting of pious women by
themselves for conversation, prayer, and collecting money,
wherever they can conveniently meet, we entirely approve. But let not the inspired prohibitions of the great
apostle to the Gentiles as found in his Epistles to the
Corinthians and to Timothy be violated. To teach and

exhort, or to lead in prayer in public and promiscuous assemblies, is clearly forbidden in the holy oracles."

With all their learning and piety those founding fathers of the American Church must have forgotten that Paul was writing about women in Corinth, and not in Massachusetts or Virginia. They might as well argue that the apostle encouraged people now to hold slaves. In his letter to the Ephesians, a sort of " circular epistle," he did not have to deal with local and temporary problems. There he wrote some of the most wonderful words ever penned about women. (See Eph. 5:27; also Gal. 3:28.) So our foremothers must have known that the apostle was not legislating about women's work in the United States. He was trying to keep the women of his day from endangering the reputation of the churches of their time.

In spite of all the hardships and difficulties, the newborn movement lived, and gradually got free from its swaddling clothes, clumsily fashioned by men who knew more about theology than about babies. After a while in their deliberative bodies these men discovered that they needed to use common sense in applying the epistles of Paul to the growing missionary work among women. As early as 1811 our own General Assembly made honorable amends for the previous attitude of uncertainty and suspicion. No doubt this action embodied the substance of a formal address. Even though ponderous, it must have delighted the " gals " of 1811:

" It has pleased God to incite pious women to combine in associations for the purpose of aiding in their voluntary contributions one or the other of the above institutions [Missionary, Tract, and Bible Societies]. Benevolence is always attractive, but when dressed in a female form it possesses peculiar charms. Hard indeed must be that

heart which can resist the example and solicitation that
are for the promotion of public good. We hope that the
spirit which has animated the worthy women of whom we
speak will spread and animate other bosoms." Now I call
that a right gallant speech!

LEARNING FROM MISSIONARIES

The work among Baptist women seems to have begun
in a different way. In China one of their early missionaries, a minister named David Abeel, became convinced
that the best way to relieve the ignorance and distress of
women and girls in China and India was to secure unmarried women as missionaries, free from family ties and
trained to teach boys and girls, while carrying the gospel
to mothers in their homes. All this may sound to us like
an old, old story, but then it must have seemed like a
startling innovation.

In 1834 this pioneer set out from China for America, to
make his plea for these unmarried women. En route he
stopped in London. There he presented the case with such
fervor that London women representing various branches
of the Church organized the " Missionary Society for Promoting Female Education in the East." This is said to be
the world's oldest interdenominational women's missionary society, and is reported to be still a going concern.

Here in America, Dr. Abeel met with an equally enthusiastic response from the women, who at once took
steps to form an organization. Then up rose the men's
boards already in operation, who " strenuously opposed "
this innovation. The women gave up the project, at least
for the time. But when once an idea of sorts gets into the
hearts of good women it germinates. Twenty-seven years
after the first abortive attempts the Baptist women of Bos-

ton formed their own organization, and during the next few decades similar groups of Baptist women formed across the country, all for the support of unmarried women missionaries in other lands.

Thus the American Baptist women pioneered in sending out single women to serve as teachers and workers among the women in distant lands. The first ones went to Burma, where they helped to carry on one of the most effective ministries in the history of modern missions overseas. Meanwhile here at home the independent women's work among Baptists met the same sort of prejudice and opposition as in other branches of the Church still obsessed with the idea of male superiority. Little by little, through prayer and faith, with courage and perseverance, those women went their way, gradually securing the approval, the respect, and even the admiration of the leaders in the men's work for world-wide missions. This way of working still prevails in the American Baptist Church. The General Board cares for married couples and single men; the Women's Board, for unmarried women missionaries in Burma and elsewhere in the Far East.

From early days the Methodist women too had their local groups to promote missionary work at home and abroad. By the time they were ready to form the National Women's Foreign Missionary Society most of the prejudice and open opposition on the part of ministers and laymen had broken down and disappeared. On March 23, 1869, in Tremont Street Methodist Church, Boston, eight women gathered at the urgent call of Mrs. William Butler, a missionary from India. She made a plea for women to teach and doctors to heal the women and girls of the Orient, to whom male teachers and doctors could gain no access.

Isabella Thoburn offered herself as an educational missionary, and Clara N. Swain, M.D., volunteered as a medical worker. The latter became the first woman physician to be sent to India. At first some of the Boston women felt appalled at the idea of providing the salaries and the equipment for these two women missionaries, together with their traveling expenses. Others with more faith and courage pleaded with their sisters not to lose the opportunity to send out two such fine representatives as Miss Thoburn and Dr. Swain. "No," said one leader, "let the Methodist women of Boston walk the streets in calico" rather than fail to hear this Macedonian call from the women of India: " Come over into the Orient and help us."

Concretely, the leaders asked every Methodist woman in Boston to do two things, which belong together: " Pray without ceasing, and give two cents a day." To us a gift of two cents may seem like a trifle not worth mentioning. Of course two pennies went farther then than now, when nothing less than a nickel counts anywhere except in church. Even so, is there in Boston, or anywhere else among us today, a denomination all of whose members give an average of $7.30 a year to world missions?

Out of such tiny acorns has grown one of the largest and most active women's organizations in the world today. In the now United Methodist Church nothing else surpasses the Women's Society for Christian Service. In every local church both men and women agree that " no woman's club can compare with this body for breadth of outlook, patriotic purpose, cultural depth, and magnitude of enterprise." This work, " of the women, by the women, and for the women, combines citizenship, international outlook, genuine Americanism, and spiritual idealism." Better still, it embodies the ideals of God's Kingdom, which is " right-

eousness, and peace, and joy in the Holy Ghost"
(Rom. 14:17).

In other denominations the women's work has grown
and prospered. In fact, with their smaller numbers some
bodies not so well known put the rest of us to shame by
their proportionate giving and the number of women missionary workers overseas. The Lord alone can tell what
the movement has meant to women and girls in the Orient
and all around the world. "This was the Lord's doing,
and it is marvelous in our eyes" (Mark 12:11). We ought
not to feel surprised, because the growth and the power
of women's work for missions shows in part the fulfillment
of Peter's words at Pentecost: "I will pour out of my
Spirit upon all flesh: and your sons and your daughters
shall prophesy, . . . and on my servants and on my hand-
maidens I will pour out in those days of my Spirit; and
they shall prophesy" (Acts 2:17, 18).

RELATED READINGS

Harner, Nevin C., and Baker, D. D., *Missionary Education in
Your Church.* Missionary Education Movement, 1942.
Hayes, Florence, *Daughters of Dorcas.* Presbyterian Board of
National Missions, 1952.
Hubbard, Ethel D., *The Moffatts.* Friendship Press, 1953.
Judd, Bertha G., *Fifty Golden Years.* Du Bois Press, 1927.
Laubach, Frank, *Teaching the World to Read.* Friendship
Press, 1947.
Miller, Kenneth D., *Man and God in the City.* Friendship
Press, 1954.
Moffett, Samuel H., *Where'er the Sun.* Friendship Press, 1954.
Philips, Harvey E., *Blessed Be Egypt, My People.* The Judson
Press, 1953.
Shaw, Mabel, *God's Candlelights.* Friendship Press, 1943.
Sloop, Mary Martin, M.D., with Blythe Legette, *Miracle in
the Hills.* McGraw-Hill Book Company, Inc., 1953.

6

AS AN INTERCHURCH LEADER

Besides everything else, the thing that burdens me
every day is my anxiety about all the churches.
— II Cor. 11:28 (Goodspeed).

DURING THE PAST CENTURY the women of each denomination tended to do missionary work in their own
way. In the first half of the present century they have
been learning to co-operate. In the years to come they
may adapt their methods to the sort of Church union for
which Dr. E. Stanley Jones, the late Sarah Chakko of
India, and others have prayed and worked. Naturally
opinions differ about whether or not we should have one
Church that embraces most of Protestantism. But whatever the future holds in store, we women ought to be
doing all we can to make the unity of Christ's body visible
to the world.

LEARNING TO WORK WITH OTHER WOMEN

Ever since 1855, Christian women have been working
together happily in the Young Women's Christian Association, but everyone knows about that. At Topeka, Kansas,
in 1898, Mrs. Charles F. Menninger, wife of a well-known
physician and mother of two foremost psychiatrists,
started a Bible class which attracted hundreds of women
and girls from all the churches of the city. The Bible class
became so influential that the date for the Governor's
Reception once had to be shifted, because the persons in
charge had unintentionally chosen the day on which the

Menninger Bible Class had its weekly meeting. In 1923, Mrs. Menninger's unique plan for Bible study was adopted by the Y.W.C.A. Since then such interdenominational Bible study groups have grown up over the country from Maine to California.

In her book *Days of My Life*, Mrs. Menninger has made clear the secret of her effectiveness: "My aim in this Bible class work has always been to make the Bible characters live, to make the Bible itself understandable and interesting to the reader. I feel that we should view the text historically, symbolically, and spiritually. I am sure it offers the best possible help to those who want to find God in their daily lives." In much the same spirit women of various denominations have been trying to help each other in missionary work without losing any of their loyalty to their own local and national branches of the Church. The methods differ as much as the stars in the sky. One of the best reports comes from a suburb of St. Louis:

"In our town Tuesday is church day. Whatever the denomination, if you plan anything but church work for a Tuesday you are almost ostracized. In our own case we meet at ten in the morning and there is an unwritten law that all meetings must close by three in the afternoon. The children take their lunches at school, and nothing ever interferes with Mother's being home before school lets out.

"During the morning one group sews; the executive board meets, and so do other committees. Anything relating to the women's work of the church is planned for between ten and twelve. At noon for a number of years the pastor's wife led a devotional service in the chapel to which everyone was invited. Then she turned the leadership over to the women, who took hold with a will. At twelve thirty a luncheon is served at cost, twenty-five cents. If anyone wants dessert, she pays extra. There is a church cook, and we all take turns in the kitchen or the dining room. We sign in, receive instructions, do our work, and sign out again. This may sound like a Detroit assembly line, but it works well and we like it. No one works more than two hours, so that we never feel all fagged out.

"At one thirty we have the business meeting. Usually the pastor speaks briefly. Then we break up in circles, except that once a month we have the regular missionary program with all the women meeting together. Oh, it is a grand church!" Yes, and it must be a grand community, for it seems that all the churches observe the same day, with something of the same live program. Later this person moved to another town, which had smaller churches and apparently little interdenominational vision. She hopes for the day when the workers in the new community will meet together and plan to make the women's work in the churches the most thrilling part of a week's program. Certainly it should be easier for churches to co-operate in a smaller town. Why not?

"The trouble here is too many traditions. The only missionary organization in our church is composed of elderly women, with the same officers and the same dull routine year after year. The same people give the same kind of programs, with a haphazard way of doing things. The pastor and his wife are trying to get some new ideas injected into the minds of the women, but so far it has been an uphill job." Of course these women need new blood and leadership. They also need to branch out and mingle with women in the neighboring churches. Until they do, they are not likely to discover why the book of The Acts is " the most exciting part of the Bible," and why missions can be the most thrilling enterprise on earth.

That plan of having a day for the women of the various churches every week seems to be a good setup. It helps to put the churches on the map, and gives a new slant for the right sort of publicity in the town papers. But some die-hard sisters will protest: " We have always had our meetings on Thursday, and we can't change now. You'll have to count us out." Really, it would do their souls good to get out of the rut and begin working with all the other church women in town. Then Presbyterians would get to know and respect United Brethren, and Episcopalians would " sisterize " with Congregationalists. This may not mean Church union, but it surely spells Christian unity, which for the present seems to be within reach.

> " In Him shall true hearts everywhere
> Their high communion find;
> His service is the golden cord
> Close binding all mankind "
> (John Oxenham. Used by permission of Erica Oxenham).

DARING TO BE DIFFERENT

Whether or not aging women like the fact, conditions do change. "Today is not yesterday." " New occasions teach new duties " almost everywhere except in an old-line missionary society, which is gradually dying out because it refuses to change with the times and with the community. As a result it fails to enlist the support and interest of younger women, who would like to try new methods in church work. The customary way of meeting such a situation is to start a new society, with members twenty years younger than in the other group. Surely the

Lord never intended us older women to huddle off by ourselves, having little to do with younger members in our own congregation, and even less to do with anyone in the neighboring churches. I have always contended that there is no age limit in Kingdom work, and experience shows that this is true in the more successful societies.

Fortunately, the answers to my questionnaire show that women everywhere are willing to experiment. In a downtown community wide-awake mothers became concerned about little children who ran the streets on Saturday afternoon and got into all sorts of mischief. The women hit upon the plan of inviting the children into a church for a free movie, followed by a Dixie cup of ice cream. The committee in charge carefully selected each film, and made sure that there were enough comic cartoons to keep the youngsters interested. As a consequence they kept the children busy and out of trouble for three hours on the one weekday when they were not in school. This is the sort of community enterprise in which the women of neighboring churches can all work together.

A writer from a small town in Maryland tells of a community project there. The men have a Lions Club, but no suitable place for their weekly luncheons. They asked the women to help them. Here again is a fine opportunity for the various societies to co-operate. In a small church the serving of weekly meals throughout the year might become burdensome. But when several groups band together, as in the Maryland town, the load is distributed. Here the men are willing and able to pay for first-class meals hot from the stove. If men from the various churches know that their money goes to all the local societies, this too makes for community spirit. Strange as it may seem, community spirit is not common in some small towns, partly because the women of the churches do not work together enough to know and care for each other.

In another town, a county seat, one of the churches has the only large, commodious assembly hall in the community. The church shows a hospitable spirit by permitting the women of any society in town to use the assembly hall, paying only for the cost of heat and light, with a small fee for the sexton. Whether we know it or not, people in the community are watching the women of our churches to see how much we love each other and work together in peace.

In our area a beautiful interdenominational work is done by the Pennsylvania Medical Missionary Society. Approximately 250 women members, representing various branches of Protestantism, are all active in their home churches. We meet once a month, and raise nearly all of the budget, $10,000, by voluntary contributions. Thus we provide scholarships for young American medical students preparing to enter missionary service overseas, and for nationals from other lands who wish to do medical work in their own countries after graduation. Some of these nationals attend colleges at home. Others who have mastered our language study here. Missionary doctors on furlough, wishing to take refresher courses, are eligible to receive such aid. If the recipient later is unable to serve as a missionary doctor, he or she repays the amount. Otherwise the money is an outright gift.

The monthly meetings are well attended and are always interesting and helpful. The speakers, as a rule, have been sponsored by the society, or now are being aided. Sometimes the nationals relate thrilling experiences from their native lands. This same group provides six cottages at Ventnor, New Jersey, for missionary families at home on furlough. The letters from these tired friends are deeply moving. Their gratitude to us for making it possible for them to step into a clean and comfortable home, is touching. Obviously the women of no one denomination could do such large and varied work. It began in a modest fashion and it has kept growing so that for many of us it has become the finest piece of interdenominational work we have ever seen.

Lining Up with Present Forces

In some cases no change of community setup may be necessary. If there is a Y.W.C.A., for instance, it needs church women ready to help with many projects for working girls. Instead of providing facilities for such work separately, the churches of a community establish and maintain a Y.W.C.A. By serving on the board of directors, teaching Bible classes, and helping in countless other ways, especially befriending homesick girls, the women of the churches in a community can do much to keep the Y from becoming merely a social club. They can also keep more than one young girl from getting mixed up with the wrong crowd.

In almost every city the churches have gone together to form a council. As with the Y.W.C.A., we may not approve everything the council does or fails to do. Still it is good for a church or a Christian woman to line up with the existing forces that make for interchurch friendliness and co-operation. In the activities of any council either a society or a single member can find something worthwhile, such as a baby clinic, a club for boys, and one for girls, a prenatal clinic, legal assistance for a delinquent lad, a home for unmarried mothers, playgrounds for underprivileged children, summer vacation church schools, summer camps, and other activities that no one church could support and direct.

When the council operates in a community, leaders of

the women's societies can take advantage of its facilities to promote interchurch activities, such as fellowship luncheons, world community day, and an interdenominational missionary institute, where the church leaders meet to study the missionary textbook that the various societies are to use later during the year. In fact, in a large city these opportunities are so many and so frequent that one has to be careful not to overdo, when the point of it all is to find peace in God.

One thing no woman or society should ever pass by or treat flippantly is the World Day of Prayer; or it may be the Week of Prayer. Through these times of war and confusion, the churches need to unite in prayer. In most communities the men expect us women to take the lead. We have been glad to do this ever since 1896, when Mrs. Henry W. Peabody and Mrs. Helen Barrett Montgomery, both of the Baptist Church, asked Christian women of all denominations to unite in a nation-wide Day of Prayer.

During the war years in Princeton our World Day of Prayer service was held in a Negro Methodist church. We met with various races and different denominations. A Negro woman was our leader. A man from Japan and another from Korea stood before us and called each other "My brother in Christ." Then each told how God's love had erased all hatred from his heart even while the two nations were at war. A Negro girl sang a group of spirituals. A Mexican girl sang in her native tongue and costume. A woman from Czechoslovakia told how God had sustained her family during their flight from Hitler. A woman from China related her experiences of what Christ had done for her country. As we sat listening to these friends from many lands, the room seemed to be charged with the power of the Holy Spirit, so that everyone could see in Christ the cure for the ills of the world at war.

In that same town the women of the three Negro churches formed an interdenominational Friendship Club. Out of limited funds they helped and cheered a number of elderly people who had no families and few friends; provided scholarships for two Negro young people away at school; and gave a prize to the Negro girl graduate with the best record in high school. These women also contributed modestly to the Red Cross, the Hospital Fund, the Salvation Army, and other benevolent causes.

At our home some members of the club met two ministers, Akoa and Chigga, who had come from the Cameroun, Africa, to study in the seminary. When they learned from " Brother Joseph " that $25 would support a girl in school for a whole year, these women immediately voted to contribute this amount. Later when Brother Joseph wrote from Africa that the Christians needed money to enlarge their church building, the Friendship Club sent another gift of money, with a picture of the members of the club. Not to be outdone, the friends in Africa wrote back that they had decided to adopt the name " The Friendship Church." As is always the case, the donors received far more than they gave.

Last year in Philadelphia more than a thousand women of all denominations and various races met in a fellowship luncheon to hear Dr. Frank Laubach. He told about his work in helping to do away with illiteracy in India and many other lands. That day the offering for his work amounted to over $1,300. Better still, many of us caught a glimpse of what our missionary representatives can do if the nations of the Far East and the Near East persist in closing their doors to Christian evangelists. With Dr. Laubach we saw the vision of teaching earth's underprivileged nations to read the Bible, and thus become acquainted with Jesus Christ.

These large assemblies have their place, but they also have their perils. Women in a small church or a small community may feel that there is no room for their kind to fit in. For instance, take an Armenian church whose women invited me to speak not long ago; or the Seventh-Day Adventist women with whom I recently met. Every community has such bodies, which may be doing religious work in their way, but still the members may feel cut off from other churches. We who have known the joys of Christian womanhood in America should learn to act as friends to the women in churches that may seem to be on the outside.

As Christian women, we ought also to show our concern about the people of other races who live near us. This may mean migrant workers in the potato fields, or American Indians across the way, or immigrants from the Far East. More likely it will mean Jews or Negroes.

Much of the inspiration for co-operation among churches, and among races, comes from what we used to call the foreign mission field. In China, in Korea, in India, and in other lands, the missionaries and the nationals have shown us how to live and serve together as sisters of the same Lord and Saviour. When we think about the barriers of caste and the ages of tradition binding the souls of women as firmly as men used to bind the feet of baby girls in China, we stand amazed at the spectacle of practical equality between men and women in those national Churches, as well as between the races. When we give thanks for our women missionaries overseas, let us also pray, " O God, help us to be like them."

II

THE WAYS OF THE CHURCH WOMAN

7

AS AN ASSISTANT TO THE PASTOR

Help these women, for they have labored
side by side with me in the gospel.
— Phil. 4:3 (R.S.V.).

A HINDU WOMAN of high caste recently spent two years
at one of our university centers, and while her husband engaged in graduate work she made a study of the
community. Before coming to the States she had formed
opinions about American homes and womanhood as they
are portrayed in films from Hollywood, as well as in popular books and magazines. Once on the ground she became more and more impressed by the beauty of the life
in our Christian homes, the charm of the women, and the
influence of the church throughout the community. Now
that she has returned to India, let us hope she is helping
to foster in her home the same sort of Christian ideals.

As Emerson used to say, at its best America excels in
women. If this Hindu guest had visited other communities, she might have found the sort of conditions she had
learned to expect, but not in any community where
women do their full share in home and church. If she
could have looked behind the scenes, she would have
found that in her temporary home town many of the
church women served informally as their pastor's assistants. Without any organization, or fanfare, they stood
ready to do everything to keep him from overtaxing his
time and strength, so that he could give himself solely to
his work as a minister of Christ.

VOLUNTEERING FOR SERVICE

In one church a woman of middle age came to her minister and asked what she could do to help him. " I am busy only in the morning; I want to be of use in the afternoon and evening. As you know, I have free use of the automobile, but I do not know what to do or how to start without interfering with the work of other women." In confidence the minister explained two matters that had been on his heart. " In the congregation we have women whom nobody is reaching. Especially in the Bible school, our women's work appeals only to those who have been here for years and years. These new people in the congregation and out in the community need someone to get them interested in the Bible, in the church, in each other. Now that's a big order, and you can work it out any way you want. All I ask is that you get permission from the leaders of the Bible school and the women's society before you start anything in the way of a group."

At once this woman began to do the sort of personal work the pastor and his wife would have done if time and strength had permitted. After the volunteer assistant had become acquainted with the newer women, both at church and in their homes, she got them together socially at her house. She found them eager to do two things: to read and study the Bible together on a weekday while the children were in school; also to go out calling on each other, on new women in the church, or on those who ought to be in church.

In another city, a woman of a different type appealed to her pastor for something she could do, something different from what she had found in regular activities, which she did not intend to shun. Knowing her bent, he told her about his shut-in friends. "I can't go to see them as often as I like, and I can't stay as long as they wish. If you and your friends will take them on your hearts, you can make them feel that neither the Lord nor their church forgets them." In this quiet ministry, she found peace of mind. Also she enlisted others to care for certain cases. As for the shut-in friends, not even a blind woman could ever feel, Nobody cares for my soul.

A third woman, whose interests leaned toward books and reading, did not find a place in the regular work, which was well organized. From the pastor she learned that there was a lack of missionary reading within the church. Of course he left to her the ways and means of distributing the material. After she had conferred with the head of the women's work, the new aide assembled two or three dozen books about missions, including some of the most popular biographies. She began to circulate these books among the women, keeping careful account of each book and its borrower. Before many months had gone that congregation became missionary-minded.

These cases had to do with individuals and with more or less specialized services. I asked the pastors what each of them most wants from church women. Only a few mention the serving of dinners, though of course that has its place. Somehow or other every minister stresses the more spiritual needs, and most of all the need for prayer and living with the Bible in the home. At the risk of repetition I give here a statement of what these men want from the women of their churches: Bible classes where women really come to know the Book and how to use it in their daily lives; prayer groups, backing up the total program of the Kingdom through the church; promoting the missionary spirit; teaching in the church school; singing in one of the choirs; house-to-house visiting; helping to integrate new members; providing for the social needs of the church and community.

These are some of the things a woman can do to help, yet we must recognize the fact that not everyone is a suitable person for some of these jobs. She may not be the one to teach a class in the Sunday school or to attempt house-to-house visiting. She may think she has quite a voice, but others notice that she sings off pitch. An overzealous or improperly trained person may force unwanted assistance on the pastor, and he doesn't always know how to cope with such an individual. As a matter of fact, one of the basic problems in church work is to convince the genuinely talented person of her ability to do the Lord's work, while finding satisfactory outlets for the energy of those who do not recognize their own limitations.

In many of our churches all the women's activities are theoretically under a central governing board. In practice, however, as long as the women go along according to approved standards, those in authority do not interfere. If some headstrong person keeps bungling the women's work, it is their responsibility, not the minister's alone, to find other ways to employ her energies. If some unpleasant situation should arise, the pastor can ask his governing board to deal with it.

A case in point occurred in a city church. A new minister had come. Out of nowhere a circle decided to raise money by giving a style show. When this word reached the minister, he called a meeting of his governing board. "Since when did this church begin to raise the Lord's money by giving style shows?" he asked them, and they told him that it had never been done before. "Are we going to begin now?" The official board, whose responsibilities include the making of policies for the church, dealt with the situation directly. They did not pass a law; they talked with people. There was no style show — and there were no permanent hard feelings among the women. So can a board deal directly with an individual who does not seem suitable for the work she is volunteering to do.

For the most part, the minister is glad when someone asks him for work. The endeavor may not be conspicuous, just as a large part of the minister's own duties consists of details that would seem like drudgery if he did not love the Lord and the people he serves. But keep looking and asking. There is a place for you.

LEARNING TO MAKE A CALL

In nine churches out of ten today the most immediate way to help the minister is to call on newcomers and on women of longer standing who feel lonely. Here again, the caller needs to have wisdom and tact, or she may do more harm than good. A pastor says: " One of the greatest gifts of Christian womanhood is cordiality. If this quality is coupled with enthusiasm for her job, she makes an ideal person to do calling in the name of the church." If she loves people, she can " show herself friendly " without being gushy or insincere. Incidentally, she ought to cultivate a sure memory for names and faces, lest she seem to " cut " the newcomer when she passes her on the street wearing a hat.

Even a timid woman can learn how to make a call. In a certain church, because of an unhappy experience when she first united, a woman with a beautiful spirit developed an inferiority complex. When she confided in an older friend, the two of them arranged to go out calling. Knowing her ground, the older woman led to a suburban district where the houses looked imposing. At the first stop the younger woman exclaimed, "My land, what are we getting into?" Once inside the door the two found themselves at home, with the new woman well worth knowing.

At the next house, still more imposing, men were laying a new hall carpet. Steering her guests beyond the sound of hammers, the hostess, still in a morning dress, made her callers feel welcome. So the shy woman concluded that wherever they may live, people are only people. "It doesn't make so much difference what sort of house people live in as what sort of people live in the house."

This younger woman soon gained confidence in herself, and by keeping at it she became a first-class caller. She never forgot when she entered a home that she went as a representative of her church. While she could have found fault, since the church had not yet reached perfection, she was always a booster. She left each home with the assurance that she had helped to strengthen the ties with the church that both women loved.

In recent years my husband and I have become fairly well acquainted with the inner workings of a number of churches. In each case we have found much to admire, but again and again we have said to each other, "At any one of our three churches the women did more calling in a month than these women do in a year." Like everything else in church work, these activities need to be carefully and skillfully organized and supervised, if only to prevent overlapping of effort and overlooking of persons. In most cases the overlooking is more serious than the overlapping.

In a community we know there are two churches of the same denomination. Each has an able minister and reasonably adequate equipment. Whenever the doors of one sanctuary are open, people stream through and fill all the pews. In the other house of worship, pews are vacant fore and aft. What makes the difference? In one case the women excel in calling and boosting their church. Newcomers like the callers so much that they come to the church with pleasant anticipations. They meet with a cordial welcome. In the other church the women do some calling, which has lessened as the months go by. They are careful to explain, " Our church does not believe this and it does not sanction that." The listeners soon decide that they have troubles enough of their own without going to a church where well-meaning people pour cold water down their spines.

Knowing that pastors rely on women even more than on men, I asked them what qualifications they most desire in such helpers. The list that follows is partial, yet it warrants study and self-examination: common sense, dependability, spirituality, evangelical fervor, initiative, enthusiasm, self-effacement, willingness to co-operate, loyalty to leaders, accepting the will of the majority, a spirit of love and compassion, willingness to make personal sacrifices, rejoicing when others do well, and giving others the praise.

At first glance the requirements seem impossible. Surely no one woman claims all these virtues, but everyone can try to attain them. Evidently the matter of Christian character bulks larger than the kind of traits that mark the leader of a woman's organization elsewhere. In church work " it is the heart and not the brain that to the highest doth attain." A closer study of the list will show that the work calls for Christian love. According to the apostle, in his word picture of an ideal Christian, love that comes from Christ includes and crowns all other talents.

ORGANIZING TO HELP THE PASTOR

We have been assuming that this kind of work ought to be done more or less individually. In most cases that would mean visiting in a piecemeal and haphazard fashion. Many women who miss the mark as callers lose their interest and quit the job. This part of women's work needs a calling committee. For ten years it was my happy privilege to serve as chairman of such a group. Some of the closest friends I have today are women on whom I made the initial call in the name of the church.

During the first year we concentrated on members of the church who either did not belong to the women's society or were not active. In later years we worked more directly with newcomers. As soon as we enrolled a new member for the society we asked one of the present members to serve as sponsor. On the basis that what is everybody's business is nobody's business, we singled out a member sure to be congenial with the newcomer, and who would act as a personal shepherd, bringing to the new relationship a warmth of friendship. If we had twenty new members that meant twenty sponsors. Each of them would call on her newcomer, arrange for bringing her to the next meeting, and then introduce her to the society.

Rising with the new member, the sponsor would tell her friend's name, with something about her husband and the children, where they lived, and anything else of general interest. At the tea following the program, the sponsor would stay by her new member, introduce her to others, and do everything possible to make the occasion an important event. If any new member asked to be excused because of shyness, we did not insist that she stand. Otherwise we followed the same procedure month after month, as we found it added interest to the meeting. The sponsor continued to shepherd the newcomer until she began to feel at home. Then she in turn stood ready to act as a sponsor.

As soon as we had eight or ten new members we arranged for a tea in one of our homes. With the new members as guests of honor, we also invited all the sponsors, as well as the pastor's wife and some of the officers. We purposely kept the numbers small so that there would be a sense of intimacy not possible in a group of fifty or more. Among the working members there came to be a friendly rivalry. " Be sure to let me serve this month as a sponsor. I want to get in on the tea." The practical result of this plan was that women not on the calling committee began to discover new neighbors living near them who had no church home. They would notify me or some other member of the committee, and charge me, " If she joins remember she is *my* new member." All of us enjoyed those teas, but no one appreciated them so much as the new members, who had been wondering how they would ever make up for the happy social hours they had enjoyed back at their former homes.

The one who has the privilege of serving as chairman of the calling committee has one of the choicest spots in women's work. Not only does she help her organization, but she lifts a great burden from her pastor's heart. One of my cherished keepsakes is a letter of appreciation from my pastor after the first year of our committee's work.

The head of the calling committee tries to persuade helpers to become familiar with the art of calling. In these days of shifting church memberships, because of comings and goings, it is doubly important to keep all the women well acquainted with each other in the church family. One way we widened the circle was to get a certain woman to drive her car. After a while a group of the younger women got together and arranged a pool of cars so that the full-time church visitor might never have to walk on her rounds. Sometimes they also did this for the pastor's wife.

Two of the women, kept at home by illness, ran a sort of clearinghouse. First they found out when the service would be needed, and then they secured a car and driver. These two at the clearinghouse kept a list of all the volunteers, each of whom stood ready on a certain day of the month, sometimes in the morning, more often in the afternoon. These young women who gave themselves with their cars were called partners, rather than drivers. The partners thoroughly enjoyed this ministry and they were always eager for an assignment. Among the discerning ones there grew a new understanding of the pastor's life and work, and hence a new appreciation for the church.

The committee went on the principle that every member of the society needed exercise, unless she were ill. Then she needed a friend or two to stand by. We tried to call in as many other women as we could. But the main satisfaction in retrospect comes to the woman who has served as chairman. Again and again some mutual friend would try to introduce a relatively new member. The latter would say, " Oh, she was my first caller when I came to town." Now that I have handed the work over to younger women I covet such memories for them. If you have a choice about which work to do, give the preference to the calling committee. If you are asked to serve as chairman, slip an extra gift into your thank-offering box.

Using Other Ways of Work

There is no substitute for calling on a woman in her home. You never really know her until you have seen her where she lives. The chairman's work is made easier if she keeps a little memorandum book for the new members and their sponsors, showing names, addresses, and telephone numbers. Even with the best of intentions, the new member may become so involved in fitting rugs and hanging draperies and adjusting furniture as to get mixed up about the date of a coming meeting.

Whenever a newcomer joins the society, you may ask her if she would like to have you call her on the telephone a day or two before the meeting. In almost every case your new friend will ask you by all means to call her. Of course the notice about the meeting appears in the church bulletin, in the newspaper, and in the folder showing the program for the year, but, human nature being what it is, you'd better take no chances. If you do not feel sure about the sponsor, phone her too, just thanking her for willingness to introduce her new member at the next meeting. If you love people, you will enjoy these friendly contacts and the chats over the phone, and if people do not like you, let the society get another chairman!

Church women ought also to make use of the mails. No mimeographed post card can ever take the place of a handshake or a smile. But neither can anything transitory take the place of a written note about the new baby, the passing away of a loved one, the graduation of a son who has earned a Phi Beta Kappa key, or the marriage of a daughter. In certain times of happiness or sorrow one may not feel like intruding, but a note, short and from the heart, shows that the friends in the church know and care when joy or sadness comes to a home.

Above all, we can pray for these new members in the society and for their loved ones. Here is a young mother who has learned that her baby boy will always remain feeble-minded, and another who has gone through the divorce courts without having done anything wrong herself, or a woman whose life has been a torment since her husband has become an alcoholic. Every such one needs the tender, loving sympathy of another woman. We can use our time and strength and substance in no better way than by ministering to those who are in sore need of comfort.

Expecting Much from the Pastor

This arrangement of having women to assist the pastor ought to work both ways. Not only should he find helpers in every good work; we in turn feel that we should look to him for what no one but a man of God can give us and our children. I hesitate to follow this line of thought lest I seem to find fault with pastors whom I have respected and loved. I have served with more than a few and have admired them all. I do not wish to criticise any of them.

Many of us feel that some ministers today do not appreciate the importance of pastoral calling and personal counseling. Just when a man is needed most he may be off attending a conference, or if at the church he is tied up in a committee. He may feel so troubled about the world's destiny as to forget the sick souls in his parish. We who are well and strong and able to attend church do not want him to punch our doorbells every month or so, but we do wish that he would spend more hours among his people, in small groups, in their homes, and at their bedsides in the hospital. As a future bishop told my husband while the two served as pastors in Columbia, South Carolina:

"When I first came to this parish I tried to help run almost every organization in town and some throughout the state. At last I discovered that if I did not serve on these committees other men would take my place, but if I did not carry out my part of the work in the home church, nobody on earth could do my work." Such a good shepherd must be a delight to the Lord, not because he is famous but because he is faithful.

When we come to church we need God — I mean God in Christ, as he makes himself known through the Spirit, and as we learn of him in the Bible. Here I can only quote the words of a strong layman, President Howard F. Lowry, at The College of Wooster in Ohio, when addressing students at Union Theological Seminary. These words mean a great deal to me because my son has since become his pastor!

"One of you, for all I know, may someday be my minister. I should want you to be in some sense an expert in theological knowledge, as I should expect expertness from a doctor or a lawyer. But the biggest thing I should want from you is not philosophical ideas about a deep consciousness of the soul of man in relationship to God. I should want you to have some interpretation of that fundamental self in every man of which most men are only dimly conscious."

8

AS A LEADER IN GROUP WORSHIP

God is a Spirit, and they that worship him
must worship him in spirit and in truth.
— John 4:24.

THE MONTHLY PROGRAM of every woman's society at
the church begins with a devotional service. So does
the less formal gathering of a circle in a private home.
This part of the work is under the care of the spiritual
life secretary, who may bear some other title. In the
yearbook of one society after another the minister's wife
is listed as filling this office. Sometimes it seems that the
women expect her to do their praying; that is, in public.
Why else does she draw her salary? As if she had any
salary to draw! Of course all pastors' wives ought to feel
that "prayer is a reality for them and that what is real
and vital they should share with other people." One of the
best ways to do this is to get other women to pray in
public.

DARING TO LEAD DEVOTIONS

Leading in group devotions is one of the highest privileges that comes to a Christian woman. Yet it is amazing
how many perfectly lovely, charming, capable women
refuse even to try. Seldom does the chairman hear a
woman say, "Yes, I'll be glad to lead the devotions."
After we left the pastorate I served as spiritual life secretary in two different churches, where many of the women
seemed to think that the minister's wife and I should

102

serve as unpaid chaplains and do all the praying. Were they afraid of being criticized? Too diffident? Too indolent to dig? Unable to find helps for leaders of devotional services? Were their own inner lives so shallow and muddy that they had nothing to share with others?

I cannot believe any of that. Many of the women were personal friends of the Lord Christ, and I feel sure almost every one of them had her private devotions at home. In the replies from laywomen some report that they too work with others who at least have desires and aspirations for better things. The pastors also express a longing for more spirituality among their women. These men seem to feel that many of the most energetic workers are not willing to serve the Lord as pray-ers. If so, the fault may be with our Protestant way of neglecting to train boys and girls for what we shall expect them to do when they are grown.

Preparing to lead a devotional service does not call for professional skill, but it does take for granted a warm and hearty experience of Christ's redeeming love. Many a woman who could not preside over a formal gathering can lead others along mystic stairs that bring them close to the heart of God. If she has a spirit of devotion, with humility and sincerity, she can share this with others. "Let the redeemed of the Lord say so."

A word of warning to any veteran in this part of the Lord's service: It is better to get ten women to lead in group worship than to do the work of ten women yourself. Often it is easier to render this service than to persuade someone else to serve, unwillingly. But do be patient, loving, kind, and sympathetic with anyone who feels uncertain in daring to take her first step. If the desire is there, the beginner needs encouragement to stand on her feet and go forward, sure of skillful hands and loving hearts, always ready to help.

"I'll try," said a lovely young matron whom I had persuaded to lead a group of more mature women. At first she declined, because she felt conscious of youth and inexperience. She was ready when the hour arrived, for of course she had ample time to prepare. A wise woman never leaves such arrangements until the last moment. When this dear girl stood before the group her heart failed and tears began to roll down her cheeks. Somehow she got through, but when she sat down she felt like pulp. After the meeting, when some of us rallied round to render first aid, we were surprised to hear her say: "I'll do it again. I will not be a slacker or a sissy." We assured her that she was neither, and advised her to wait awhile. Later I had an exquisite little note in which she said her newly discovered faith was so intimate and precious that she just could not yet expose it to public view. However, she was determined, with God's help, to bear witness in public. She later became an active leader in the young married people's group.

Another goodhearted woman of middle age assumed the presidency of the missionary organization. She had many other marks of leadership, but she never had tried to pray aloud in the presence of a group. At the proper time for the prayer before the luncheon she started out bravely, faltered, started again, and then came to a sudden stop. With face distorted in anguish, she turned to the woman beside her and sobbed: "Oh, you do it! And I had such a nice one thought up!" Before the next meeting she had evidently made a different sort of preparation; when it came time for the prayer, she went through it without a hitch, a genuine overflow of her thanks to God.

Making a Plan for Devotions

The tyro in such matters may not see why she has to make plans as carefully as for a birthday party at her home. Especially when brief, a period of devotion needs one central motif. In turn this depends on the type of meeting and on the season of the year. We do not plan to dress or to serve food the same way in June as in January. Before Christmas a leader may think in terms of the Christ-child, and during Lent, about the meaning of the cross in Christian experience today. With some one purpose clearly in mind she may begin by selecting the hymn. There is time for only one, and that one ought to be in keeping with the spirit of the entire service.

In the choice of a hymn look for the kind of song that appeals to the young women whom the society is trying to interest as active members. We older ones may prefer to sing " The Sands of Time Are Sinking," but the younger women are more likely to love the words and music of " Joyful, Joyful, We Adore Thee," or the Christ-centered beauty of " Fairest Lord Jesus." After you have selected your hymn be sure that the woman who will play the piano knows the music and can lead in the singing. If the pianist is not skilled, it is better to choose something simple like the Chautauqua hymn, " Break Thou the Bread of Life."

One can find as much enjoyment in choosing a hymn to suit the spirit of a devotional as in selecting the proper hat to go with her gown. Not everyone knows how to do either! On Mother's Day, an organist selected the hymns for the morning service. Later she complained to the visiting minister, "I couldn't find a single song in the hymnal about mother except 'O Mother Dear, Jerusalem.'" If that girl had lived fifty years ago and had chosen the hymns for the funeral of a man's third wife, she might have used the words, "Passing away, one by one."

After the hymn may come the Scripture reading. While short, it need not seem insipid. According to the season of the year, and the purpose of the hour, select something that makes complete sense, such as a psalm or a parable, as well rounded and beautiful as an exquisite cameo. Do not shy away from the old favorites and do not be afraid to introduce a Bible passage that others may never have heard. Search the Scriptures until you find something short, impressive, and beautiful. Prepare to read it so that others will feel about it as you do.

When I was a girl in a country school, I learned that one may read too quickly, or monotonously. Sometimes the teacher would tell one of us to select and read a Bible passage the next morning. When she asked me to do so, I rushed home and begged Father to help me. He suggested the closing chapter of Ecclesiastes, which isn't exactly the easiest part of Holy Writ to interpret. He told me to find the passage in the family Bible and read it aloud. He coached and corrected me, until he saw that I knew what it meant and how to get it across to others. That night I prayed for God to be with me.

Between four o'clock that afternoon and nine the next morning I must have read those words aloud at least fifty times: "Remember now thy Creator in the days of thy youth." I found that chairs made an admirable audience. They were so serene, so uncritical! Ever since then I have tried never to read before others until I have gone through the passage aloud and prayed about it in private. Before he opened his mouth in public Booker T. Washington always talked things over with God. As a lifelong lover of the Bible he could have said with an old-time "leader of worship": "Neither will I offer . . . unto the Lord my God of that which doth cost me nothing" (II Sam. 24:24). This is an excellent rule for anyone who wants to become a leader in worship.

A good reader knows how to make the words of the Bible sound real. What John Wesley said about certain ministers holds true about some of us women when we try to read what we do not feel: "Somebody ought to pay them to keep quiet."

A solo or other special music may come after the reading. A leader does not plan to use her own voice prominently in two successive parts of the same service. She wishes as much variety as possible. If she cannot secure a singer, there may be a violin solo, perhaps even a harp. Consecrated musicians render such services as acts of worship and not as entertainment. They feel embarrassed if people burst into applause, and irritated if women start to whisper. The right sort of person does not wish the leader to cease worshiping God while she tosses verbal bouquets to the guest artist.

No group of women would applaud at the end of the pastor's prayer. It is an act of worship offered to God. Well, so is a sacred song or an instrumental solo from Mendelssohn or Bach. If musical selections are not sacred they have no place in a devotional service. As for a social gathering, the artist may sing a number of secular songs after which the group should applaud, whether or not she deserves it. But when she dedicates her gifts in a time of group worship, explain the theme of the service

and ask her to sing something more nearly Christian than
" Brighten the Corner Where You Are."

Preparing to Pray in Public

We all shrink from making prayers in public because
we feel uneasy about our own limitations and shortcomings. We forget that our God is able to deliver us from
such fears. We have Christ's promise to his disciples when
they asked him, " Lord, teach us to pray." " If ye then,
being evil, know how to give good gifts unto your children; how much more shall your heavenly Father give
the Holy Spirit to them that ask him? " (Luke 11:13).
No Spirit-filled woman ever should refuse an opportunity
to lead others in prayer. In one of George Eliot's moving
stories a woman character testifies:

" It is such as I — the helpless — who feel themselves helpless — that God specially invites to come to him, and offers all
the riches of his salvation. Not forgiveness only — forgiveness would be worth little if it left us under the power of our
passions — but strength, that strength which enables us to con-
quer sin."

One way to overcome timidity in group worship is to
pray aloud in private devotions. Then one becomes accustomed to the sound of her own voice. The difference
is that in private prayers one's thoughts may wander, and
then one can pray about what has come into the mind.
In a group one needs to keep on a single path of thought
and feeling, so that others can follow.

Most of us write out our group prayers, word for word.
Then we feel sure of being coherent and intelligent, and
not being heard for our " much speaking," with the kind
of vain repetitions that we employ when unprepared.
Personally, I have never read a prayer before others that

I have composed. I do write one out. If I want to read a prayer, I look for a collect (accented on the first syllable) such as the one ascribed to Chrysostom. This collect, and many other forms suitable for group worship, appear in *Prayers for Services,* by Morgan P. Noyes:

"Almighty God, who hast given us grace with . . . one accord to make our common supplications unto thee; and dost promise, that where two or three are gathered together in thy name thou wilt grant their requests; fulfill now, O Lord, the desires and petitions of thy servants, as may be most expedient for them; granting us in this world knowledge of thy truth, and in the world to come life everlasting [through Jesus Christ our Lord]. Amen."

It seems better, I think, not to choose the same sort of prayers and other forms of worship that the minister uses on Sabbath morning. In an hour of public worship he tries to express all the worthy desires of the people in the sanctuary, and of their loved ones everywhere. So he may follow the old acrostic, which calls for these elements and in this order, but not all in any one prayer. Adoration — Confession — Thanksgiving — Supplication — Submission (for service). In group worship there is not time to include all of this. One simply wishes to lead the group into the presence of Christ our King, and leave them there. How simple, and satisfying!

DELIVERING A DEVOTIONAL TALK

Like each of the other parts, the devotional talk ought to be short. Usually the time allotted for everything is fifteen minutes. Do not run over. Time everything. Be careful not to rush. When ill at ease one often speaks too rapidly, sometimes indistinctly, even incoherently. Be deliberate, but don't dawdle. What is not heard or grasped can do no good. In five minutes, or seven, one can say a great deal if well prepared. But it is harder to outline a brief talk than a longer one. Jesus made a single point in each of his parables, and he made that one strike home to the heart because he spoke simply.

When you stand to speak, hold your head up and look at the group before you, eye to eye. Remember then that they love you and wish you well. Be sure to stand still and refrain from fluttering your hands. Of course you will be carefully groomed, with nothing flamboyant or bizarre. This is not a style show or a hairdo exhibit. Speak out so that everyone can hear. In *King Lear* when her father referred to Cornelia's voice as "low," he must have meant in pitch and not in volume. "Her voice was ever soft, gentle, and low, an excellent thing in woman."

The ability to make oneself heard depends on careful articulation rather than loudness. At a railroad station in olden days everyone could hear the train callers bellowing like bulls, but with never a word that made sense. A woman needs the sort of voice that carries. Here and there a woman ought to tone down and soften her nasal twang so as to speak more gently and more quietly. Most of us ought to learn to speak out so as to be heard by the semi-deaf individual who persists in sitting back, where she complains she cannot hear.

One such fretful listener learned that the pastor's wife was to conduct the devotions. With customary frankness she said to the other woman, "Oh dear, your voice is so soft nobody will hear you." Without resenting such a tactless remark, this wise woman replied: "Yes, I know that my voice is soft. I wonder if you will help me. If you sit back in the room halfway I'll watch you. If you can't hear me, just put your hand to your cheek and I'll speak louder." The partly deaf woman felt pleased at being asked to "help," and the leader knew that if this particular hearer sat halfway back, and could catch every word, so could all the others in the room. Whatever you do, "carve every word before you let it fall." When you have finished your part, close your books quietly and leave the platform. If you drop a book or stub a toe at this point it will spoil the effect of an otherwise satisfying period.

One of my correspondents asks me to stress the unwisdom of chewing gum while leading the devotionals! "We have a good woman who is a tireless worker. When she leads the devotions she reads a couple of verses from the Bible, and then champs on her gum, looking off in the distance and ruminating. [What creature is it that ruminates most?] Then she reads another couple of verses and repeats her part of the act. It is all I can do to sit still." No wonder! A later report says, "Mrs. _____ was re-elected president and she still chews gum!" Instead of laughing at this misguided woman, the spiritual life secretary can ask her privately to park her Juicy Fruit outside or, better still, leave it at home.

Careful attention to details is necessary in order that the whole period may be Christ-centered. No one present can think about him and a blundering leader at the same time. Neither can any guide in such worship feel sure of escaping criticism. A deeply spiritual friend was leading the devotionals and was lifting us up to the gates of heaven. An old sister in the audience who always spoke in stage whispers croaked: "Why doesn't she hold her head still?" Some of those present were ready to lay hands on the critic!

If one is tempted to say, "You can't please everybody,"

let her remember that she can render sacrifices pleasing to Him, and to his dearest followers. By his grace, and without special training in schools, any one of us can claim the words written about the coming Redeemer:

" The Lord God hath given me the tongue of the learned, that I should know how to speak " (Isa. 50:4).

The following devotional, prepared by Mrs. Frank S. Niles, Bryn Mawr, Pennsylvania, illustrates the ideals of this chapter.

THANKFULNESS FOR LITTLE THINGS

Call to Worship — Psalm 100:4.

Prayer: O God, who dost call us into thy presence, help us now to come through thanks and wondering joy till we behold thee as thou art. Through Jesus Christ our Lord. Amen.

Scripture — Colossians 2:6, 7, and 3:16.

Meditation — Can Paul mean that thanksgiving may be an entrance into strong and abounding faith?

A very lovely friend who is blind once said, " I think we miss so much of life, all ready for us, because we forget to give thanks for the little things."

So I began to think about some of the little things for which together we ought to give thanks. The strength that comes from food; the delight of sharing with others a thought or an experience; the refreshment of laughter. The warmth of sunlight, and a friendly room; the touch of snowflakes on the cheek; water plentiful and near. The texture and the pattern of life, all wrought from little threads.

Then too the little things that God has entrusted to us:

tasks not to be despised; opportunities never to be taken for granted.

"As ye have received Christ Jesus the Lord, so walk ye in him," remembering how God has honored little things through him in whom all fullness dwells. The little town where he was born; the little children he blesses; the flowers he told us to consider. The seed that he promised would remove mountains; the little loaves and fishes with which he fed the thousands; the grain of wheat that would live again. So we give thanks through Jesus Christ our Lord.

Prayer: O God, our Father, who givest grace for grace, who makest faith to grow out of thanksgiving, we praise Thee for the multitude of little joys through which thou dost touch our days with glory.

May we watch for them with eager expectancy, and receive them with adoring praise. May we find in them the beauty of the sweetest sounds, repeated often, and accepted with thankful hearts, till our lives sing with thy melody, through Jesus Christ our Lord. Amen.

Let us now sing, "For the Beauty of the Earth."

RELATED READINGS

Applegarth, Margaret, *Right Here, Right Now*. Harper & Brothers, 1950.

Brown, Ann Curphey, and Glis, Sally Brown, *Handbook for Group Leaders*. Womans Press, 1950.

Crowell, Grace N., *Devotions for Women*. Abingdon Press, 1953.

Crowell, Grace N., *Riches of the Kingdom*. Abingdon Press, 1954.

Grimshaw, Ivan G., *How to Prepare a Speech*. Womans Press, 1952.

Kerigan, Florence, *Inspirational Talks for Women's Groups*. The Standard Publishing Company, 1951.

Laman, Nedick A., *How to Speak the Written Word*. Fleming H. Revell Co., 1949.

Rest, Friedrich, editor, *Worship Aids for 52 Services*. The Westminster Press, 1951.

Trecker, Audrey and Harley, *How to Work with Groups*. Womans Press, 1952.

Vining, Elizabeth Gray, *The World in Tune*. Harper & Brothers, 1954.

Wagner, Russell H., and Arnold, Carroll C., *Handbook for Group Discussions*. Houghton Mifflin Company, 1950.

9

AS A PLANNER OF CHURCH PROGRAMS

For we are laborers together with God.
— I Cor. 3:9.

THE EFFECTIVENESS of work among women hinges on the program committee. Here we shall think mainly about the chairman, taking for granted that she enrolls other members as workers. We may also assume that she has some weeks between her appointment and the time when she takes up her tasks in which she can make plans and let them mature. In planning church programs, just as in preparing to speak or to pray, "time is of the essence" of the contract. Without worry or excitement she can study the local field and the world situation, survey the forces at hand, assemble her materials, and gradually work out a program for using these resources.

Some societies plan to cease activities in May and do not resume work again until October. This seems to me a mistake, because the fall plans do not really get under way for a month or six weeks afterward. The treasurer is begging for funds, committee work is slow in getting started, and interest in general lags during the long vacation. If the new planner of programs is on her job, she will try to prevent anything like a slump during the warmer months. Summer meetings can be different from the ones in winter, but they need not be dull.

SETTING UP A YEAR'S PROGRAM

First of all the chairman may send a letter to denominational headquarters asking for literature about various programs. Naturally they have more to do with the work at large than with the methods of a particular society. But the local leaders must not ignore these suggestions about people and countries far beyond our ken with more or less detail for mission study courses. From the same sources the chairman can secure names of missionaries on furlough who are available for presenting special causes.

While materials are coming through the mail, the program maker can study printed or mimeographed copies of what the society has done in previous years. Tentatively she can decide which of the former items to adopt, in different forms, and what new features to add. For instance, in past years have there been many imported speakers or only a few? How should they be spaced? How can the society keep a balance between the work at home and the work abroad? Many of these answers are dependent on location. A group near a furlough home for missionaries may rely too largely on speakers from outside. One far away from such fountains of missionary information may not have enough visiting speakers. Usually it proves more difficult to secure speakers about National Missions than about the work overseas.

A year's program will prove worth as much or as little as it has cost in securing information, in using common sense about what to do with the assembled materials, and in giving all this a kind of lift with prayer. As one heaven-sent leader said about the way another built her program, " Somehow she always plans for the glow and the sparkle." Her missionary meetings became known among women as just as interesting, as informative and as up-to-date, as those in any woman's club in town.

The subject for one meeting may be Japan or Korea. In recent years the society has had a number of speakers from the land under discussion. Unfortunately, some of the ablest mission workers may not have the sort of imagination that can take the wings of the morning and transport the hearer to distant scenes. Through the "grapevine telegraph" the chairman needs to learn, not only which speakers are available, but which ones can use words to paint pictures. In lieu of such a speaker from the outside, let the chairman plan her own meeting. This is especially needful where the society has been suffering from "speakeritis."

The program about China or India may have "eye gate," as well as "ear gate." From her friends the planner may secure pieces of embroidery, scrolls, vases, pictures, chopsticks, and many other articles that will make the meeting seem unique. These may be used as decorations. Better still, she may keep some of them under cover, with the covers plainly in view, until the time comes to answer unspoken questions. Women like to watch the opening of surprise packages. If someone can explain a piece of art from China or India, or appear in costume, that will add interest to what another may say about the work among women over there.

All this takes time and thought, but is anything less good enough for God? Once our committee decided to set apart a meeting to promote the use of the denominational missionary magazine, which we rated first-class. We arranged for a series of living pictures. One of our young people made a large frame with a door to simulate the

front cover page of our magazine. The sexton arranged
to throw a spotlight on this doorway, and during the
meeting the rest of the room was in darkness. From time
to time the woman in charge opened that mysterious
doorway and presented a person from one of the fields
where our church was at work. Another made a brief talk,
full of facts, about the work represented by the one who
was standing in the doorway.

There stood an American Indian woman, a mute witness to the sufferings of her people at the hands of white
invaders. Next came a Mexican girl in costume, her eyes
pleading with us for what religion has never given girls
in Latin America. Again a group of Negro men were
posed, representing the statue of Booker T. Washington
lifting the veil of ignorance from the faces of his people.
We saw in succession a woman from Japan, one from
Korea, and another from our Southern mountains, all of
them living reminders that the sun never sets on the
workers we help to support. We had good reason to
know why we ought to read our magazine. In this sort of
program the effectiveness does not depend on the skill
of the artist who makes the door, nor on the women who
pose in colorful garments. The idea calls for a sense of
reality. Simply show the facts " drawn out in living characters."

After the meeting an enthusiastic friend said to the
woman sitting beside her, " What a lot of time and
thought the chairman must have put into the preparations for this meeting! " " Oh, yes, I suppose so," was the
reply, " but she didn't have to do it all." Indeed not! We
had a live committee and we planned to use as many
other women as we could, especially those who had never
taken part in any program. Some of the women whom we

persuaded to pose would not have taken an oral part in a program, but they were willing to be seen without being heard. They felt a new concern about the association because they had taken active parts in one of the unusual programs. We kept the immediate objective in sight, so that we secured a number of new subscribers for our missionary magazine.

The program committee should not permit some introvert to stand up and mumble a reading from a magazine, after she apologizes, " It is so much better than anything I could say myself." No matter how good it is, such an article always seems to be a leftover not even heated for the occasion. In order to forestall such extemporized monotony be careful how you choose those who will carry out each program. If the woman has had experience, and knows how to plan, let her alone. If she is inexperienced, she may need some coaching. This kind of teamwork goes on in private. When the meeting time comes, the woman in charge gets credit for an interesting and helpful program. The next time she has to work out a plan she knows better how to begin. Thus the home society becomes a training school for future leaders.

" Woman's work is never done." Surely this holds true of the person in charge of program-planning. She and her committee not only make the plans and invite the leaders or the main speaker, but the chairman holds herself responsible for the success of every meeting. Through the person in charge she checks all the details concerning the hour — a lot of trifling items that one never notices unless they go wrong. As a boy said about salt, " It makes the potatoes taste bad when you leave it out." His mother may have a bad taste in her mouth after she attends a missionary meeting where things happen higgledy-piggledy. But when all things work together for good, according to a plan, the same woman wants to come back and enjoy the next meeting.

PLANNING FOR VARIETY

Every homemaker knows that her family require a balanced diet. Not only should her meals be balanced, they should also offer variety. At home she may serve potatoes several times a week, but not always sliced in the same shape or cooked in the same style. If she comes to a church meeting she may ask herself why it always has to be the same. " The women of our church must love our pastor. In our meetings the leaders try to do what he does on Sunday. Why can't we have a change? " You can, if you get a wide-awake program committee. With only ten or twelve meetings of the entire group each year, an alert committee can arrange for that many different ways of representing " the drama of redemption."

Dorothy Sayers, of Britain, used to write mystery stories, sure-enough thrillers. Now she is writing essays and books on Christianity. She declares that there is more mystery and drama in our religion than in anything else on earth. She would feel astounded if we American women, with all our wealth of resources, could not present missions in dramatic and thrilling forms. If anyone asked her how to do it, she would reply: " Use your imagination. That's what it is for — to serve God, from whom it comes."

Mrs. Roy Koten, of the Evangelical United Brethren Church, Indiana, shows how to use imagination. She is writing in *The World Evangel* for the women of that Church. " Two years ago our theme was Latin America. In my local society the first meeting was a *fiesta*. We carried armfuls and auto loads of things to our meeting, so as to create atmosphere and interest. We played Latin American games, our waitresses were in costume, and our luncheon menu was symbolic. Throughout the afternoon we used Brazilian music intermittently. Two of our ladies presented the need in Latin America through a role play. One acted the part of a wealthy Brazilian woman, the other an American Protestant missionary. It was exceedingly effective.

"When it was all over and the same things had to be carried back to the cars, one of the women who had shared a great deal of responsibility murmured: 'I just don't know whether it was worth all this work.' Just then one of the new members rushed back into the room to get a book. 'My goodness,' she exclaimed, 'I learned so many things I had never known before. I wouldn't have missed it for anything. You really made it seem like an occasion.' The tired woman looked at me and smiled. Yes, it had been worth all the effort."

Another meeting centered around the work of the denomination of Ybor, Tampa, which members of the society should visit when they go to Florida. Again a meeting focused on India. The women brought in Oriental rugs, set up an open market (Oriental plan) in one corner, and sprinkled rose water on each woman's hair as she arrived. One of the members tied a wreath of paper flowers loosely around the neck of everyone who was to take part. After she had tied the last knot "with an enthusiastic jerk," this flower lady looked at the program chairman and almost shouted: "Mrs. X, do you lie awake at night thinking up things for us to do?

Indeed she did. How else would the women come to feel close to the Indian people? "You see," explained

Mrs. X, "we are trying to pave the way for Helen's book review on *The Christian Needs in India*." At the end of the meeting, packed with still other novel ways of doing old things, the woman who had fashioned the wreaths of flowers said to a friend: "Wasn't this an enlightening meeting? Why, I feel as if I had been in India." So it proves, as Mrs. Koten says, that "we learn from hearing, that we learn more from seeing, and that we learn most of all by doing."

If every society had such a chairman for the program committee, there would be endless variety in the meetings, and endless profit to all.

RELATED READINGS

Ely, Virginia, *A Book of Installation Services*. Fleming H. Revell Co., 1954.

Haller, Ruth, *Planning Your Meeting*. National Publicity Council, 1953.

Sorenson, Roy, *The Art of Board Membership*. Association Press, 1950.

Strauss, Bert and Frances, *New Ways to Better Meetings*. The Viking Press, Inc., 1952.

Trecker, Harleigh B., *A Manual on Recruiting and Holding Effective Board Members for Your Organization*. National Publicity Council, 1954.

Weis, Auren, *How to Be a Successful Leader*. McGraw-Hill Book Company, Inc., 1953.

10

AS CHAIRMAN OF A CHURCH MEETING

"Let all things be done decently and in order."
— I Cor. 14:40.

THE CHAIRMAN of a church meeting feels responsible for its success or failure. If she has personality, skill, and tact, she can bring out all that is good in a worthwhile program. She can also ease strain and prevent any embarrassment. On the contrary, even the nicest blunderbuss can spoil the best-laid plans of the most thoughtful committee. So the committee carefully chooses the woman who will carry out each program. Leader and program go together like the words and tune of an inspiring hymn. The chairman leads in presenting the program, and the program gives the chairman pleasure. When she knows her business, she thoroughly enjoys this part of the work.

As soon as a woman learns of her appointment as leader, she starts to get ready. She looks up telephone numbers and lists the people on whom she will call most frequently. She keeps a pad of paper near the telephone, jots down each detail that she ought to arrange, and checks off the parts that she has delegated. As the time for the gathering draws near she decides what to wear. The dress must depend on the person, the season, and the occasion. It should be pleasing, rather than flashy, and near enough to the current mode not to attract the eye either of envy or of criticism. If anyone happens to be distracted by the length of the skirt, the fashion of the hairdo, or any other detail, that fact is unfortunate, inasmuch as the leader's appearance could have as easily seemed just right.

"Carefully groomed" is what I mean. In every detail from the tip of her toe to the crown of her head the chairman is ready to stand before her group so that they will think only about Christ and his work. Superfluous and often unconscious movements show that a woman is thinking too much about herself. Before she goes to her meeting she ought to kneel down in her bedroom, placing herself and her meeting in the hands of God.

KNOWING THE RULES OF ORDER

This complicated business of presiding needs preparation; a woman who presides must know how. This demands the careful study of a guidebook in parliamentary practice. Every society ought to own such a volume, which the secretary may keep. This book should go into the hands of every leader who will preside over any meeting, unless she already knows the rules of the game. Even if she does, a review may help to refresh her mind. In one sense of the term a leader of a meeting is not "born with a knack," but is "trained for a privilege."

The following meaty suggestions come from one of the best books for inexperienced leaders. In his *Basic Rules of Order*, Thomas H. Eliot omits many of the dry details that fill some of the older manuals. He makes things clear to a person who is neither a lawyer nor a member of Congress. His suggestions are for "doing things simply and quickly, with common sense instead of rigid formality, but always within the limits of good order and fair play which underlie the Rules themselves:

"A *quorum* is the number of members, or the percentage of the membership, whose presence is required for the transaction of business." Every organization should decide what number will make its quorum at business meetings. Usually one fifth of the membership should be enough. Every leader ought to have this information clearly in mind before she takes charge of the business session. If in doubt let her consult the secretary or some-one who knows.

"The one *making the motion* should be recognized by the chair. The seconder need not be. A motion made and seconded makes a matter open for discussion or debate. If done in an orderly way, much pointless discussion is avoided.

"An *amendment* may be proposed during the discussion. The proposer makes a motion to amend the first motion. If seconded, and carried, the amendment is voted on before the main motion.

"A presiding officer's primary duty is to preside in a manner that is firm, polite, and scrupulously fair. She will most easily perform this duty if as chairman she exercises the qualities of patience, dignity, and impartiality.

"Firm self-control — the ability to remain, or at least appear, perfectly calm and unruffled under difficulties — is of course nearly vital to the maintenance of a chairman's dignity, and of great importance to the whole meeting." (From *Basic Rules of Order*, by Thomas H. Eliot. Used by permission of Harcourt, Brace and Company, Inc.)

After she has made a preliminary study of such a book, a would-be leader keeps her eyes open. When she attends a meeting somewhere else, she enters into the spirit of the occasion. When she goes home, she tries to recall what the chairman did, and what she didn't do, in making the gathering an "occasion" and not merely an occurrence.

Every woman ought to preside in a natural way, which is never like that of a man who pounds the gavel. But every chairman should be as well informed about the rules and as impartial at all times as the referee of an athletic contest.

Through the years I have admired the way different women have presided over various kinds of meetings. In one respect I have usually found them all alike. Time after time I have gone home saying to myself: " She always says the right thing and does the right thing in the right way. When she stands up in front of us she looks happy. She seems to be having the time of her life. She loves to preside." I first knew such a woman chairman in my dear sister, Dr. Anna P. White, an outstanding leader in the women's work of the United Presbyterian Church — a great missionary Church. For her example of radiant Christian leadership I still thank God.

After the chairman has mastered the rules of order she may need to reflect on the spirit of her new responsibility. She will find this in Paul's prose poem on faith, hope, and love. The chairman sets the reality behind these words as her goal. Whenever she presides she will give an example of what the love of Christ means embodied in a Christian gentlewoman today. To put the same thing differently, she will preside according to the rules of order as they are " interpreted by love."

PREPARING A CAREFUL DOCKET

Every gathering of any size requires a carefully prepared docket, written down in black and white. Even a committee meeting with only three members goes along better if the chairman has decided in advance what matters ought to come up and in what order. The leader prepares her docket before the hour of meeting. Almost every assembly of any consequence may have to consider matters about which the chairman ought to know beforehand, so as to be ready to lead in suitable action. The docket may run like this:

> Brief devotions
> Minutes of the last meeting
> Reports of permanent committees
> Reports of special committees
> Report of the treasurer
> Call for the offering
> Opening for new business
> Motion for further business
> Program for the day
> Motion to adjourn.

To keep all these details in mind and in order, the presiding officer needs a loose-leaf notebook of modest size, perhaps five by seven inches. She may keep this within easy reach at home so that she can write down all the items that will come up, and the sequence in which they will appear. In presiding over a meeting one's love of order is as vital as it is in being a good housekeeper. Even with the best memory a woman needs a self-reminder or what is sometimes called a " tickler " system. A group of women become fidgety if the chairman has to scrabble through a pile of odd-sized and variously tinted papers, hunting for some elusive reference. The chairman will follow the right path if she thinks out her course at home — if possible, while the children are at school or sound asleep!

A different sheet may contain items that she must take care of, and then check off, before the meeting starts. This includes seeing that the person who is to play the piano is present, ready to begin playing a few minutes before the hour. Then too someone ought to check with the sexton to see that the room is aired, properly lighted, and neither too hot nor too cold. The right number of chairs and hymnbooks, and no more, should be in the right places. In these little things one tries to make the church home seem "homey," especially to strangers.

Should something of a technical nature or a delicate issue be coming up, the chairman ought to write in her notebook what she plans to say. If one makes an exact record of what is to be reported, there is a measure of self-protection against later criticism. If called to account, the chairman can turn to her notebook and feel sure about what she has said. There is nothing equal to a written document to spike hearsay or rumor. Such occasions, however, seldom arise.

A careful chairman sets her watch correctly. She plans to start exactly on the hour, and to close on time. In planning she allows so many minutes for the devotionals, so many for business, and so many for the program, with a little leeway for the long-winded. If there is to be a guest speaker, the chairman plans to deal with routine business, if possible, in some other way, so that the speaker will have enough time, instead of having to address a group already bored by reports from a dozen committees.

In order to have everything move on time Mrs. Able plans to be on hand fifteen minutes early. Without seeming to "snoop," she checks as unobtrusively as possible to have everything in order. She sees that all who have any responsibility for the day are present or accounted for. If anything unexpected arises at the last minute she can delegate somebody to take care of it. She looks as gracious and unfluttered as a hostess in her home, with never a worry in the world. This is as wholesome, and as rare, in a group of twenty as in a gathering of two hundred. In either case the hour calls for poise, charm, and radiance. For all these reasons the chairman plans to arrive at the place of meeting with a rested body and a mind at peace.

How different are the ways of Mrs. Unable! We have already noted that she has arrived late at her first meeting. After singing "the first and last verses" of a hymn, she asks a member to lead the devotionals, which consists of stumbling through a few ill-chosen verses from Hosea (where *is* Hosea?), reading a sentimental ditty, and asking the group to "repeat" the Lord's Prayer.

As Mrs. Unable rises from her chair to go on with the meeting, she clutches at the rear of her skirts and twitches them into place, then slumps over the desk, and says: "I guess we should have the business meeting now. Is there any business coming up?" (She certainly does not know of any!) A member proposes some business and makes a motion, but Mrs. Unable does not know how to put the motion. She asks: "Is that the way you want it?" She sees nods of assent and says: "Well, I guess that's the way it is." When the times comes for the program, the women are engaged in a free-for-all debate about whether to have pie or ice cream at the church supper. That critical problem too is settled by the "guess so" method. If this seems overdrawn and silly, I can testify that I sat and suffered through that meeting. A good chairman never guesses. She knows!

INTRODUCING A GUEST SPEAKER

Somebody ought to write a booklet on "entertaining angels unawares" (Heb. 13:2), and a copy ought to be given to every chairman of a woman's society. She alone does not do all the entertaining of a guest speaker, but she can do much to make the weary missionary feel at home among friends. People often forget that although the visitor serves under the " Board," she still is a human being, whose body isn't made of India rubber. Sometimes after a year of furlough, spent mainly in deputation work among churches, a missionary wife and mother has to go to her parents' home and get a rest before she starts back overseas. To be blunt about it, a year of furlough often proves more wearing by far than the same length of time spent on the mission field.

How can the women who invite the missionary to speak help to make it a pleasant experience? The letter of invitation should go out early, possibly several months before the meeting. The writer should state the place, the date, and the hour of the day (remembering that time zones differ, and that daylight saving time is not used everywhere). The letter should also give some clues to the kind of gathering expected to hear the address. Is the group large, small, or of medium size? Will those present consist solely of women? What age group will probably attend? Should there be a set address or an informal talk? Is there a film strip or movie projector available if wanted? Does the society pay traveling expenses, and is there an honorarium? If so, how much? Never ask a missionary or a minister, " How much do you charge? " " The Lord loveth a hilarious giver," who doesn't ask embarrassing questions.

About a week before the time for the gathering the speaker should receive a note telling who will meet her, and exactly where. Do not expect a tired woman to find her way about in a strange place; she may be a world traveler, but she would much prefer to have a guide to her destination. Once a guest speaker in a metropolis received a letter telling her to take the West End bus (four blocks from where she was staying), ride to the end of the line, cross over the tracks and take the streetcar named Far Hills, ride to an intersection with a shopping center, get off, and walk two blocks. " The church is right on the corner. You can't miss it. I'll be there watching for you." The speaker was supposed to get home by the same circuitous route at eleven o'clock that night. Most widely traveled speakers can tell about being caught in a similar maze of thoughtlessness.

If the speaker lives in the same area, someone should arrange to call for her and take her home after the meeting, unless she indicates that she will furnish her own transportation. Perhaps she could find the church unaided, but it is more comfortable to come into a strange group if there is someone familiar with the place to lead the way. If all this seems too much bother, perhaps we should make a resolution not to invite a speaker whom we cannot entertain as an honored guest. Nobody likes to be treated as if she were honored by being permitted to speak to the group! " I was a stranger, and ye took me in " — into our homes, into our hearts. When we take better care of our speakers, we sometimes get better speeches.

If the speaker comes from out of town, the same courtesies should be extended at the bus or train station, or at the airport. Make sure that she has ample time before and after the meeting. On account of erratic travel schedules, she may have to come earlier in the day; or she may have another appointment the next day which makes it necessary for her to remain overnight. If this is the case, there should be a home ready to receive her. Nobody without experience can tell how much of blessing a missionary brings into a home where she is guest. But do not ask her to sit up entertaining you when her bones are aching for a bed.

As for the meeting itself, the guest arrives before the hour, escorted by a member of the society. The chairman extends a hearty welcome. If she does not already know the facts about the speaker, the two may retire for a minute or so until the chairman learns all that she needs to know. Somehow the presiding officer makes the guest feel at home. The program allows ample time for her to present the work dear to her heart. The speaker knows in advance, and so does the chairman, whether or not there are to be questions from the floor, with general discussion. Usually there is not time.

A good chairman excels in the art of introduction. She tells the facts about the speaker — such facts as will interest the hearers and prepare them for the message. If the speaker is a woman, the facts may include something about her girlhood home, her college, her lifework. One should remember that the speaker is being introduced, not her husband or children, though naturally a few words about the family are in good taste. There is no need for praise. Neither should there be any jokes of the "I remember her when" variety. Sometimes the introducer supplies unintentional humor. Once before a foreign group the person in charge said to the winsome speaker: "The aroma of your presence preceded your coming." When the words got through the puzzled interpreter, they ran this way: "We smelled you before you got here!"

In some cases the introducer talks more about herself than about the guest. "I first heard her . . . I saw her in Bombay on my last trip around the world . . . I feel sure I speak for all when I say I am glad I am here tonight." I, I, I — as though the commandment read, " Thou shalt love thyself more than thy neighbor." The audience ought to learn two things: Who is this person, and what has she done for her Lord? If the speaker is a man, the same thing goes. He wants the people to know a little about who he is, what he has done, and why he is here. After that he may speak for himself.

Sometimes the chairman introduces the speaker by making a speech of her own. She wants to demonstrate how much she has gleaned from the columns of the *Encyclopædia Britannica.* Again, she may refer to the coming address as " a little talk." She may fumble the speaker's name, or make some oblique apology for her age. It takes a speaker ten minutes to recover from such a douche of cold water down her spinal column. Any speaker knows that if she doesn't strike fire in the first few minutes, she may as well go on to the appointment in the next town.

Once in a while we feel disappointed after an address which has not lived up to the chairman's prognostications. The presiding officer said after an address: " Before she spoke our distinguished friend asked me to explain that she is suffering from temporary indisposition. I did not do so then, but I think I should do so now." Of course *that* chairman was a man! But why does a good speaker sometimes flop? Perhaps because we keep her sitting on one hip and then the other, while we fritter away time reporting in extravagant detail about which hymn the group sang last time, and what verses Mrs. Q read so beautifully before Mrs. J led in prayer, followed by Circle Four's serving refreshments consisting of tea, nuts, mints, and toothpicks!

To forestall any such waste of time some societies have the secretary post the detailed minutes, which are necessary for the record, on the bulletin board in the entrance hall. There too appears anything else of more interest to the group than to the speaker. This saves the making of reports that gobble up time. The chairman announces that the bulletin board contains these items for everyone who wants to examine them. Not one woman in a dozen glances twice at the bulletin board, yet it is there for anyone who wants to check a matter of particular interest. Meanwhile the leader's attitude seems to say: "We are here on important business. We have present one who can help us. Let us give her the right of way!"

The chairman may help, gradually, to bring about a reform. Fewer speakers and better ones! At any rate she can make sure that the guest receives a note of thanks after she reaches home, perhaps feeling discouraged over her experience. Not every speaker has the "gift of tongues," but everyone has feelings that respond to kindness. Sometimes laywomen do not know that the speaker who charges handsome fees receives more notes of thanks than the one who is taken as a matter of course, because she offers what she has to give "without money and without price."

Some of these things may seem small or unimportant. If so, get in touch with one of the leaders in your best community organization. Ask how the officers invite and introduce a visiting speaker. The persons in charge of the program do not ask just anybody, but when they extend an invitation, they treat their guest royally. As a former member of such a group, I much prefer the meetings of church women, and yet I have sometimes wished that we who plan for church meetings and preside over them would take our duties as seriously as do the leaders of an up-to-date civic organization.

RELATED READINGS

Cruzan, Rose Marie, *Practical Parliamentary Procedure.* McKnight & McKnight, 1953.

Eliot, Thomas H., *Basic Rules of Order.* Harcourt, Brace & Company, Inc., 1952.

Glass, Joseph A., *How to Plan Meetings and Be a Successful Leader.* Merlin Press, 1951.

Husted, Helen, compiler, *A Chairman's Guide.* The Reader's Digest Association, Inc., 1944.

Routzahn, Mary S., *Annual Reports and How to Improve Them.* National Publicity Council, 1951.

11

AS AN INSPIRER OF CHURCH WOMEN

She openeth her mouth with wisdom;
And in her tongue is the law of kindness.
— Prov. 31:26.

EVERY GROUP of church women needs more than one
inspirer. An automobile runs because it has a number of spark plugs under the hood. On an athletic team
one of the girls keeps the other players full of pep. If she
drops out to serve as inspirer in a new-made home, the
other members of the team may lose their interest. Without zest, a game seems hardly worth the effort. The
pastor's wife may serve as an unofficial inspirer, but not
even she can provide pep enough for all the work of the
church women. Now please do not ask me to define the
word "pep." I know what it means when I see someone
who has it.

In a certain town two women often worked together,
one as the helpmeet of the minister and the other as a
private in the ranks. After a while the two of them moved
away. A number of the remaining friends wrote: "Something is missing since you left us." "There is a big hole
here we do not know how to fill." "Our meetings have
lost much of their enthusiasm." In every church where
the women's work lags, there may be a call for a slogan:
"Wanted, a lost enthusiasm." Alas, there is no sort of
"ready-mix" that I can recommend, no short-cut way of
providing enthusiasm. Still I have a few suggestions for
anyone who feels the call to be a "self-starter."

DISCOVERING HIDDEN TALENTS

Each women's group has more than one member with hidden talents. If anybody told such a one that within a year or two she would serve as an inspirer of a circle, and later as head of the entire society, she would think the speaker ought to visit a psychiatrist. What Russell Conwell told us when I was a girl still holds true. Here in the home society, among women who may seem to themselves drab and commonplace, there are " acres of diamonds." " A worthy woman who can find? for her price is far above rubies." That is the sixty-four-dollar question! Notice the word *find*. We must try to discover a way of bringing out personality treasures.

Such a woman came into one of our churches, a real " prospector." She did her full part, but felt that she should let younger women take more of the lead. In a Bible class that she taught her eyes fell on a young Mrs. Smith, who never dared to open her mouth in the presence of the group. One morning the older woman went to Mrs. Smith and asked her to take the class on a day when the teacher had to be absent. Mrs. Smith felt appalled, but the older woman persisted, with offers to help. Mrs. Smith agreed to try and was ready when the hour came. From that time onward through the years she went from victory to victory, all because somebody believed in her and led her into active service.

In more than one church that I know, the women's work has drifted into the doldrums — " a part of the ocean near the equator, abounding in calms, squalls, and light, baffling winds; . . . A state of listlessness, ennui, or tedium." What has happened when a society gets into this kind of mood? Perhaps a few women keep the control in their hands year after year, and leave the others the unspectacular jobs. Because of the " doldrums " one woman answered my letter:

" A few women in our group feel that the heavens would fall if they did not stay at the helm. They are beginning to learn now that there are others just as capable. The pastor's wife has been insisting that we ought to use a larger number of women in our programs, and when we ask them, the leaders are surprised at what the newer workers can do. They never before have been given a chance."

Not every woman has such abilities. Many of the finest rightly feel that they can work better in other ways than in group leadership. So the inspirer needs a sort of divining rod, to feel sure where hidden treasure lies concealed. For encouragement she may read about the way Jesus dealt with young Simon Peter. Long before that hotheaded fellow had learned to harness his God-given powers, the One who knows the human heart said to Peter, " Thou art the Man of Rock." At a time when Peter was acting cocksure and yet fickle, the Master believed in him, expected great things from him, and by such belief drew out his talents as a leader. Later on when Peter said, " I go a fishing," the other disciples answered, " We also go with thee."

Recently a new woman came into a church and discovered that the leadership of the association was confined to a chosen few. In that large congregation the men's work was well organized, and she knew that the women had equal ability, though it was for the most part unused and undiscovered. The leaders did not mean to be selfish; they were merely shortsighted. " With tact and gentle perseverance she prevailed upon these exponents of government-by-the-few to try an experiment for a year. During the next twelve months every woman member of the congregation was asked to take some part in a public program. These parts were carefully fitted to the interests and abilities of the individual, so nobody had reason to feel embarrassed or frustrated.

" Scarcely a woman failed to carry out her assignment. Some who had served habitually only in the kitchen found new avenues of usefulness. As a result, throughout the women's work there was a new stir of interest, a new respect for another's ability, and a new confidence in unsuspected powers."

This is what it means for a woman with the " seeing eye " to act as an unofficial inspirer of potential leaders. If women's work in your home church seems to suffer from the " doldrums," start in as a self-appointed inspirer.

Still another church has a unique way of discovering gifts and possibilities in new members. At the close of the church year all who have joined the congregation in the past twelve months put on a special entertainment. A man who has already shown qualities of leadership serves as chairman. He gets the group together and asks each of them to tell his talent for entertaining. One plays a banjo, another a drum, a third a violin, and a fourth an accordion. These form an " orchestra " — not quite on a par with the New York Philharmonic, it may be — but certainly interesting to hear. Another has a fund of humorous anecdotes, while others agree to put on skits. The boys and girls who have joined sing a group of songs.

This entertainment is under the auspices of the women's organization. There is no attempt to provide an intellectual feast. The idea is to have an evening of good, wholesome fun that all the church members can enjoy as a family. When people laugh together, they begin to feel acquainted. After the program there are refreshments, consisting of punch and cookies. There is no stress on money, but a plate is left in a conspicuous spot and nearly everyone makes a contribution.

During the evening the women leaders of longer standing watch for special talents, and then file the information for future use, perhaps with the nominating committee. This same church has a lodge out in the country, with facilities for picnics, youth services, all-day women's meetings, and other outdoor activities. Here too the women have opportunities to discover new talent for group leadership. Under this plan there have come increasing numbers of leaders to the whole church.

STIRRING THE INDIFFERENT

We might set up as Problem Number One the large proportion of women church members who have little to do with our work. Usually it is easier to get a newcomer actively interested than one who has long been a bench warmer, and as likely as not a faultfinder. The newcomer wants friends, with a feeling that she is both desired and needed. She wishes to belong. The indifferent woman has formed her habit patterns without reference to the women's work of the church. How can we win her over?

Suppose we try the gentle note. An indifferent woman cannot be stampeded into action any more than a sensible girl can be swept off her feet by an impetuous suitor. The genuine lover resorts to strategy, and if he does not succeed at first, he tries again until he convinces the maid that they are meant for each other. And so they are married and "live happily ever after."

In courting a woman for church work one has to arouse

and foster interest. A person who has found in church a joy and delight can scarcely understand why all the other church women do not feel the same interest. We plainly have to accept the fact that they do not. Then plan to get them interested in some way, however small. Once two of the biggest businessmen in our town spent an hour trying to get a prominent surgeon interested in the Y. M. C. A. so as to make a gift of money. At last they got ten dollars, but they also " got their man," who became the leading financial supporter. He later served as president just because those two visitors got him interested in their cause. They did not use pressure, but gentle persuasion.

There is no cut-and-dried pattern for stirring the uninterested woman. One must use a different approach with every person. A woman may pride herself on belonging to the intelligentsia. If she is inveigled to attend a woman's meeting at the church, she may look down her nose and say with a sniff: " How bourgeois! Nothing in that to uplift me! Why do they not make these monthly programs as stimulating and challenging as in our woman's club downtown? "

In a certain city church the inspirer found such a woman, brilliant, and with the sort of ability the work needed, but without a spark of interest. When approached by the prospector for talent in leadership, the other woman said frankly: " I am not interested in missionary work. Even if I were, I should want programs better than the stuff I endured the other day."

So the visitor did two things. First of all, she persuaded the women to plan for monthly meetings that would appeal to those who like to bring their minds to church. She also asked other members to call on this indifferent woman and tell her how much they were enjoying the missionary programs. " They stimulate our thinking." She began to discover that the members of her church included more than a few women as well educated and cultured as she was, and every one of them spoke enthusiastically about missions.

Then a situation arose that called for the sort of temporary leadership she could supply. She was asked to help. The new project appealed to her. When she got into this part of the women's work, she found there was far more of depth and power in church activities than she had ever imagined. When at length the project was completed, she made her report before the society. The women praised her for the splendid work she had done. Being human, she liked that. She met with such a friendly welcome and intelligent response that she began to feel a desire to take a more active part.

Ordinarily it is not wise to put a woman in office who has not won her place by serving for a while in the ranks. But this person had demonstrated her ability in a difficult piece of work. A member of the nominating committee proposed her name for an office. Others protested: " She will never accept." " Certainly not," said the inspirer, " unless we ask her." After much debate the committee voted unanimously to make the experiment. To their delight and surprise she accepted. Once in office she became an informed enthusiast about the ongoing work of the society. Why do we not try more often to rouse the indifferent woman from her lethargy?

EXTENDING HOSPITALITY

Another sort of inspirer can promote hospitality. In the New Testament she finds exhortations to excel in this

Christian grace: Be " given to hospitality " (Rom. 12:13). Be " a lover of hospitality " (Titus 1:8). " Use hospitality one to another without grudging " (I Peter 4:9). In these days of eating out at hotels and restaurants, because of limited space or lack of time for preparation at home, somebody needs to promote hospitality in the church.

The inspirer of hospitality may have to begin with the kitchen. (The renovation of the kitchen is almost invariably the forerunner of redecorating the Christian education building and the church.) In most church buildings, except those of recent construction, the kitchens were planned or perpetrated by men who knew nothing and cared less, it seems, about making things convenient for the women. The place is often small, dark, and sometimes even smelly, because of poor ventilation, or none at all. The stove is antiquated and frequently out of order. The dishes, pots, pans, and the facilities for washing them also seem to have come down from antiquity. There is no steam table to keep things hot, and if there is a refrigerator, half the time it does not work.

At home we women try to have convenient kitchens, even if not streamlined, and we endeavor to keep them shining and sanitary. At church the women have to crowd into a small space, prepare and serve a meal on dishes cracked and chipped. In spite of the handicaps, be it said to their praise, they serve delicious meals! I speak feelingly on this subject, for it has been my lot to work in such kitchens.

In church we hear sermons about " the holiness of things secular," with illustrations about Brother Lawrence who " practiced the presence of God " while washing his pots and pans. George Herbert has a poem called " Elixir," where he bids us women to make our kitchen " drudgery divine." The prophet Zechariah sings about the day when "the pots in the Lord's house shall be like the bowls before the altar" (Zech. 14:20). That will hold true when women can work together in a church kitchen with quarters as comfortable and convenient as businessmen have in their offices. But in a cramped kitchen where everybody gets in every other body's way, and one steps on another's toes, and tempers become frayed, sometimes followed by hot words, the melee makes it hard to join later in songs of adoration to God "from whom all blessings flow." I have sometimes wished that certain male idealistic speakers could sweat it out behind the scenes with us women at a church supper, where these dreamers may reproach us for being like Martha, "cumbered about much serving"!

After we women have cooled off we may conclude that we ourselves are partly at fault. We may have inherited the outmoded kitchen with its helter-skelter assortment of mid-Victorian equipment. So did some of us when we came into the houses where we now live, but we brought about a change even if it took a while. With the right sort of inspirer, any private kitchen or church cooking quarters can be made over so as to meet the needs of those who often come to the family table. If we must eat our way into the Kingdom — and it seems we must — we ought to provide the workers in the kitchen with quarters and equipment as up-to-date and convenient as in any modern home. If the men in charge will let us, we can do the planning for such facilities. They will let us if we have an inspirer to plead our cause.

Each church has its own plan for promoting hospitality. In one body with 800 members a woman is appointed hospitality chairman. With the help of her committee, they envision what is needed in the way of quarters and equipment. As soon as feasible the chairman leads to the sort of working conditions that change drudgery into delight. She has the responsibility for planning the teas, receptions, dinners, and other social features of the congregational work and life. Through her committee this chairman sees that every social function has a capable hostess, but the chairman herself serves as a sort of super-hostess.

Between times the supervisor needs to keep her eyes on the kitchen equipment. The dishes and silver, the linens and cutlery, the pots and pans, with all the gadgets and gimmicks, have a way of disappearing, not because church women are larcenous, but because they are careless. Without offending sensitive persons, the chairman needs to devise ways and means to stop officious sisters who borrow from church shelves, and to retrieve or replace articles " lost, strayed, or stolen." So our chairman serves as a sort of glorified chef, without pay, and sometimes even without thanks. If she has a sense of humor, she may post the following notice, neatly typed and cheaply framed:

"Knives, forks, spoons, and napkins are not medicine. Please do not take after meals."

If there is a church cook, the two women co-operate, as in an old-fashioned home where a maid and her mistress work together in harmony. They plan the menus and work out the countless details of shopping and management. If there is no paid helper, the responsibility falls on the chairman and her committee. She needs to know everything domestic, and how to be angelic. How to cook and set a table; how to see that order reigns in the kitchen and dining room; how to direct amateur waitresses full of willingness but not having studied under Emily Post; how to keep peace among perspiring kitchen workers; how to meet an emergency when the ice cream fails to come; how to wait patiently until the invited speaker has arrived; how to bring into a church basement the atmosphere of home and the spirit of serenity.

ACTING AS GREETERS

Some churches appoint a committee to serve as " greeters " for the morning services. In a congregation with many newcomers, and more than one entrance and exit, a timid woman may enter and leave without a friendly word. If she is in quest of a church home, the visitor may never return.

Two or three alert women out in the lobby can spot any woman who does not feel at home, and have her led to sit with some friendly person. Others here and there through the congregation can greet newcomers after the services. In many churches women have learned how to be cordial without seeming effusive, both before and after morning worship, and never a whisper to interfere with reverence in the sanctuary. So many lonely women live all about us today, and they often come to church without finding what their hearts desire.

As we have already seen, in order to serve as one of the Lord's liaison officers on the lookout for new women, one needs to be cheerful and cordial. Someday one may try to shake hands with an empress dowager who is making her annual pilgrimage to the church, and does not wish to be bothered. The greeter may hear, " I have been a member of this church for forty years! " " How splendid! " says the welcomer. " I have been here only twenty years, but don't you think it's about time for us to get acquainted?" Of course it takes more than that to pierce the armor of such a matriarch. So the greeters devote their time to women who want to be sure of a welcome. Often we pride ourselves on having a friendly church because we love to visit with each other, and we ignore the outsider as though she were an intruder.

BRINGING BEAUTY TO THE SANCTUARY

A different sort of ministry, equally beautiful, is that of the flower committee. The woman directly in charge of the flowers for the chancel or pulpit platform needs to believe in "the holiness of beauty." She ought to have a sense of balance and proportion with an eye for harmony of colors. She needs to take time for arranging the flowers in their holders. If all the stems are the same length she can shorten some of them so as to have variety in height. The size and shape of the vase are important, something suitable to the flowers. There is far more to making a pleasing arrangement of blooms than just sticking them in a vase. Even with the most gorgeous flowers a bungler can ruin the effect by careless or hurried work. Lovers of beauty and harmony out in the congregation may be tempted to come forward and rearrange the flowers!

In some churches the weekly bulletin gives prominent notice about friends who have donated the flowers each week. The chairman of the committee keeps a calendar with spaces for each Sunday, so that anyone may volunteer to provide flowers on a certain "memorial" day. In response to my questions one woman reports that in her church a red rose, in the center of the Communion Table, announces to those present that another little baby has come to bless a Christian home in the congregation. Some of us used to question the fitness of flowers on the Communion Table, until we remembered that "in the place where he was crucified there was a garden."

In other churches the women budget a definite sum for flowers. Many have gardens at home, and gladly bring whatever the committee may wish in the way of floral offerings. However lavish, no display from the greenhouse can surpass in beauty the skillful arrangement of home-grown flowers, or in late autumn a setting of gorgeously colored branches from trees.

After the hour of worship the "flower lady" and her aides carry these gifts to the sick, the shut-ins, and the sorrowing. Many parishes of the Protestant Episcopal Church have a lovely custom of sending to the sick the altar flowers to which is attached the following card:

> "These flowers from the altar of St. Mary's Church are sent to assure you that you are remembered in the prayers offered there. May they bring you something of the peace and blessing of God's house."

If conditions in the home warrant a visit, it is often better to keep the flowers until the next day. People who are ill or in distress may have far too many callers on Sunday afternoon, and then none at all until the next "day of rest," when there comes another deluge. When our Lord said, "I was sick, and ye visited me," he must have meant on a weekday.

One good woman in a hospital said to my husband: "I am glad you came to see me on Tuesday. I had twenty-two callers on Sunday and it took me all day Monday to get rested." No doubt those visitors thought they were doing good when they invaded that sickroom, with descriptions of much worse cases they had known. The thoughtful flower lady learns to present her gift, listen more than she speaks, keep her voice down and her hands off the bed, and she leaves before long except when visiting a shut-in who wants her to stay and chat. A shut-in person may not have had twenty-two callers in six months. Her heart grows hungry for news from the outside world.

Even more of beauty and grace enters into the work of the Altar Guild. In some churches the women take care of all the preparations for Holy Communion. This means preparing the altar cloths, spreading the altar in spotless white, and doing everything that will enable the officiating minister to serve " in Christ's stead." After the celebration, when worshipers have departed in silence, the members of the Guild remove the vessels, altar cloth, and napkins, and restore the altar to its proper state according to the season of the year. Our Episcopalian friends have set an example for us all:

" Realizing the privilege of serving as God's housekeepers, each member of the Altar Guild should dedicate herself and her work as an offering to God, to whom nothing but the best can be given. Perfect cleanliness and punctuality are absolutely essential in God's house and are the external manifestation of the spirit of loyalty and devotion."

In a church that has an altar rail or a Communion Table, male members usually render these services. In most cases they would gladly give way to a group of women who have a sense of reverence in handling the sacramental vessels. However inexperienced, these women ought to know better than to arrange the table or the altar after worshipers have begun to arrive; or afterward begin to assemble the individual Communion cups while some of the people remain in the sanctuary. As in a well-regulated home, the women in charge of such things plan to do them as inconspicuously as they can. When people come to be "guests of God," both before and after the experience at the Lord's Table they need silence, not distraction. At the first Holy Communion, with only twelve in attendance, our Lord sent two of them before him to make all things ready for the feast.

So it seems that every society needs one or more inspirers, who can gently lead other women into all kinds of loving service.

> " A Persian fable says; One day
> A wanderer found a piece of clay
> So redolent of sweet perfume
> Its odor scented all the room.

> " ' What art thou? ' was the quick demand
> ' Art thou some gem from Samarcand . . . ? '

> " ' Nay, I am but a piece of clay.'
> ' Then whence this wondrous sweetness, pray? '

> " ' Friend, if the secret I disclose,
> I have been dwelling with a rose.' "
>
> (Author Unknown)

RELATED READINGS

Jones, E. Stanley, *Growing Spiritually*. Abingdon Press, 1953.

Perry, Edith W., *An Altar Guild Manual*. Morehouse-Gorham Co., Inc., 1950.

Rockwell and Grayson, *Complete Flower Arrangements*. Doubleday & Co., Inc., 1947. Beautifully illustrated in colors.

Spry, Constance, *The Simple Art of Arranging Flowers*. The Thomas Y. Crowell Co., 1953.

Wyon, Olive, *The Altar Fire*. The Westminster Press, 1954.

12

AS A RAISER OF CHURCH MONEY

I entreat Euodia and I entreat Syntyche
to agree in the Lord.
— Phil. 4:2 (R.S.V.).

IN BOTH HOME AND CHURCH many of the women's problems have to do with money or the lack of it. One writer
says that the Scriptures teach more about money than
about almost anything else. Anyone can see for herself
that practically half our Lord's parables deal with money
or possessions. The members of the Early Church at
Jerusalem ran into their first serious trouble because of
money, as it related to women of two different races. (See
Acts 6:1–7.) Today there are women with two different
attitudes toward raising money for the church. The same
Holy Spirit who led to a solution of the woman-money
problem in the church at Jerusalem is waiting to guide
us in dealing with church money this year and next.

GETTING THE FEEL OF THE SITUATION

"How do your women raise money for the church?"
In reply to this question a number of pastors begin by
saying, "It has long been the custom here . . ." One of
them writes: "This is a rural community, and having ice
cream suppers, strawberry festivals, turkey dinners, etc.,
to raise money has been a long-established custom. However, we are working on the idea of stewardship and systematic giving, and the idea is beginning to take hold. I
approve these things as social events. We have grand

times when we meet at one of these gatherings, but I don't believe the Lord wants us to raise his money this way."

Like many of his fellow pastors, this man is taking a sensible view of things. If with his desire to promote stewardship he had tried to squash all those festivals and dinners, he might have found himself in hot water. In fact, he might have had to move so that the women could dispense with their self-appointed pope.

The plan of raising money by selling good things to eat works better in a rural church than in a city church. Farmers' wives raise their own berries and bring them to the church festival. The same goes for chicken and turkey, with all the other items that make up the most delicious food in the life of the community. If farmers and their families eat some of their own produce they like it all the better because they enjoy it with friends who live miles away, and who never get together except at such a time of jollity.

The customs of a country church may carry over into a city congregation. Women raised on the farm keep on liking to do what they did back home. They find it harder when they have to buy everything at twice the price they used to get for the sale of farm produce. So a difference of opinion is likely to grow up in every city or town congregation. Some women want to have a good time while earning money for local expenses. They seldom advocate such means of raising money for missions. Other women line up their arguments against continuing what they call country ways of doing work in a city church.

In older times one group would form a Ladies' Aid Society. The other would organize a missionary society. Not feeling strongly convinced either way, many church women would join neither group. Now that all the women in the church are coming together and forming one united association, the issue still remains. Which of the two ways shall the association endorse and follow? Before we try to formulate an answer let us listen to the arguments from both sides. Let me frankly confess that I belong on one side, but I can see the other point of view. If it prevails, I shall honestly try to do my share. A church woman is a poor sport if she accepts the will of the majority only when she gets her own way.

HEARING FROM THE MONEY RAISERS

Replies to my questionnaires point to the fact that in country and city alike some women and a few pastors still believe in old-fashioned rural ways of raising money. In city churches the methods vary, with bazaars and other entertainments assuming a larger place than out in a crossroads village. Here are five of the most convincing arguments for money-raising projects.

The Financial Argument. "Frankly, our church needs the money. This is a prosperous community, and all the people round our church profit from its being here. None of them would live in a neighborhood where there was no church. Some of them send their children to our Bible school. Whenever we have a church social we give all our neighbors an opportunity to help us. In this way we women raise money to help the men keep the church as well painted and as attractive as any farmhouse in the community. From all accounts our neighbors like our way of raising money. They always come, and often bring along some friends."

The Domestic Argument. "Many of our farm women have little money of their own. Last year the women's organization raised more than a thousand dollars for the church. If we had tried to give that much, not counting our regular Sunday contributions, that would have been an average of more than ten dollars for each of our members, and that's more money than most of us have. City people don't realize how little cash comes into some farm homes between crops, and how small a part of it finds its way into the hands of the wife and mother. Out of what she handles she may have to buy all the clothes for herself and her children. She says that she can use butter and eggs to bake a cake that will make your mouth water, and that her husband isn't going to count the cost of the chickens that ' enter the ministry' through the church home."

The Social Argument. "Women out on the farm are busy people. We don't have neighbors next door, and we live on a half section of land a mile long and half a mile wide. We work hard. We don't have an eight-hour day — we're thankful if we get an eight-hour night for sleeping. It does us good to get together at the church. We joke back and forth when we are paring the potatoes and cooking the dinner. We like to see our families eating at the same table. We know each other pretty well, and by working together we keep our friends."

The Community Argument. "With new people coming in to take the place of those who move away, we need some system of getting acquainted and keeping our community spirit alive. The consolidated school is a long way off. Our only place for coming together is at the church. How can we get people out unless we feed them? Every neighborhood needs a social center. We have one in our church. If we quit giving suppers, what will take their place in building up a friendly, co-operative spirit? "

The Bible Argument. "We love our pastor, but some-times we don't understand his way of explaining the Bible. When he talks about the tithe he seems to forget that it started among Hebrew people and that they were farmers. Back then farmers and their wives paid their tithes and freewill offerings in farm produce and not in money. When they moved to town and tried to put the business on a money basis, they got into trouble. Over in Africa, India, and other lands, so the missionaries tell us, women bring in farm produce. Why should it be right for them and wrong for us? We never yet had a minister who refused to ask God's blessing on our food — and from the way most parsons eat, we feel they can't be too much opposed."

Where the system of money-raising prevails, it ought to abide by certain principles of Scripture. The Bible for-bids the short weight and the unjust balance. "Gospel measure" seems to mean a full dish, with "good measure, pressed down, and shaken together, and running over" (Luke 6:38). Country women pride themselves on their reputation for feeding guests well, but time was when city women were guilty of serving oyster soup with a teeny bivalve floating around in a puddle of blue milk.

In bazaars at city churches one may have to pay high prices for cheap goods, such as greeting cards one would not wish to send to her worst enemy; extracts with dim and questionable flavors, because "the church gets fifty per cent of the sale price"; silver polish that will not polish silver or anything else; tasteless and unholy candies; flimsy mops, weird little gadgets called something like Dizzy Duzzits, and other articles that nobody else in town could sell.

At well-managed bazaars women bring their own handi-work. One may not be able to give money, but one has a talent like that of Dorcas (Acts 9:39), who made coats and garments for the glory of God and the good of the church. Surely the Lord is pleased with such tokens of love when offered for sale at a reasonable price, but not when an apron goes for twice as much as it would cost downtown. "It's for the church, you see." No, I do not see how God can bless cheating in the name of the church.

The worst abuses sometimes appear at a rummage sale, which may mean the church's going into the secondhand clothing business. Is it quite "cricket" to sell for gain what has no value for one's self? "There are good reasons for selling clothes to poor but self-respecting people, provided that the profits are used for other relief among the needy, but to exploit the needs of poor people in order to support a church is neither self-respecting nor Christlike."

The Good Will Industries conduct their business on a plane distinctly Christian. A similar plan operates locally where churches maintain a "Co-operative Store," which runs a rummage sale continuously. Anyone, church member or not, whether rich or poor, is invited to bring or send for sale any article no longer needed. For instance, when we moved into an apartment we gave this society articles that were not worthless, but for which we had no room. Our congregation has two such collections a year. All the proceeds go to some benevolent institution, such as a hospital, which the donors may select. With conservation of resources on behalf of the needy, God is well pleased.

A fascinating book, *Miracle in the Hills*, by Dr. Mary Martin Sloop, tells how she and her doctor husband went into the mountains of western North Carolina and started with next to nothing. Seeing the need of warm clothing for the mountain people who could not afford "store boughten" clothes, she persuaded her friends all over the country to send in used garments. Opening a tiny store, she sold these clothes at a price high enough not to offend the mountain people. With the proceeds and other gifts from outside, those two erected building after building until at last they had twenty-five, all on a beautiful campus, made possible largely through rummage sales.

Every church woman who tries to raise money can learn a lesson from Dr. Sloop. She saw that the people had no infirmary. Soon after, she heard a sermon on Ps. 127:1, "Except the Lord build the house, they labor in vain that build it." Mrs. Sloop took the schoolboys up the hill and showed them the site for an infirmary. She had no money, but she told them, "The Lord will provide." She read Psalm 127 with them, and had another woman worker lead in prayer. Mrs. Sloop then asked the boys to start digging for the foundation. Soon the checks began to come in, some of them large, some small. Mrs. Sloop kept on praying, working, writing letters, until she saw the infirmary completed and paid for. In a sense all these buildings stand as a monument to a woman's faith.

LISTENING TO THE OTHER SIDE

Those of us on the other side cannot answer some of these arguments. Let me simply state a number of reasons for thinking that in a typical church, especially in a city, the women should not depend on money-raising projects to meet the budget. Without making any accusation against other women who are as good as gold, "as for me and my house," we will give the tithe and freewill offerings.

The Financial Aspect. Through the years my husband

and I have known all sorts of churches in all parts of the land. We think of their financial policies as admirable, not admirable, or somewhere in between. Perhaps we have observed with prejudiced eyes, but still we have never seen an admirable church where the people did not rely on voluntary giving. Neither have we ever known a congregation that seemed to us admirable where the women earned most of their money. As for the ones in between, usually they tried to serve the Lord both ways.

The difference appears to be that when women team up with the pastor and other men in promoting the tithe and freewill offerings, the stress falls on the work of the whole church, not just a part of it, and on the giving of one's entire self. More than once we have watched something that approached a revival because women had learned the joy of making sacrifices for missions. We do not recall ever having seen any such marked spiritual results from the bake sale idea. On the other hand, in a church of that sort, with high-minded women, my husband conducted more than one funeral brought on, as he supposed, by undue bodily exertion on behalf of the church.

In a city the churches may become known to the merchants as beggars or parasites. The store manager smiles, but he puts posters into the sales display reluctantly, sells charity items grudgingly, and has to take a joshing from the man next door about making kickbacks to the church. The officers of the women's society may feel proud because of the list of donations from " the butcher, the baker, the candlestick maker," but if they could hear what the merchants say when they have left, they would make fewer such appeals. The women may gloat when they undercut prices of shops in the neighborhood, but should the church, with its buildings free from taxes, enter into competition with stores whose overhead must be taken from the markup? Anyone familiar with the situation today can see enough exceptions to the rule; however, it seems fair to say that women of a normal city church ought to raise money by giving rather than by begging.

The Domestic Angle. We wives who have always controlled a fair portion of the family income feel sorry for any woman who must resort to other means. We wonder, though, if the domestic argument does not refer to women of yesterday more than today. Even though the income for a given year may fall off, the tithe takes care of the change because it is based on *proportionate* giving. When income goes up, the church should be the first to benefit, as a sign of thanks.

From our point of view a woman should not become a slave bending to the whip of a money-raising project. We can scarcely expect hard-working women to keep on working hard when they come to church. Let them rest and relax for a change. Every woman needs to slacken the physical pace as she grows older. We ought to see fewer funerals of women old before their time, because of overwork for the church!

In a congregation that we still love, one of the women came to my husband with something approaching a complaint. "You know that I do all the housework for my husband and four growing children. In the afternoon I take a little rest. Then I like to change my dress, and go out and see sick and shut-in friends for the church. Some of the other women tell me that I am not loyal. I ought to be helping them make money. We aren't rich, but I pay the tithe and a thank offering, too, sometimes. I think my work at home gives me all the dishwashing I need. When it comes to church work, I like to spend my time with people who need and want me."

What would you have told this woman?

The Social Impulse. This I have never been able to answer. Some of our dearest friends, who are dedicated ministers, believe in and practice tithing. Still they advocate some of the other ways of raising church money. "How else," they ask, "can you get women to know and love each other so surely as to have them engage in work that they can do well together?" To me this one reason carries more weight than all the rest of them thrown into the balance. Serving meals and joining in other group activities are important, but they can provide just as much fun for everybody if they are not spurred by the profit motive.

Think of a family eating dinner. Suppose the mother begins to add up the cost of the meal, harping on the price of beef, the cost of dairy products, and the way the supermarket catches her coming and going. She talks of almost nothing but money — how much she has spent, how much she will be forced to spend for food. Frequently I have heard the same thing happen in churches that eat for profit. Now suppose that the home economist plans her meal simply but tastefully, and says nothing about the cost. The family relish the food, and everyone joins in the chatter of table talk. Apparently they give little thought to the total rung up at the grocery. They are too much interested in one another. Which of these two meals would prove more enjoyable? If the latter, why not carry the same spirit of liberty over into the larger family known as the home church? In other words, as nearly as possible, keep the cash register out of church gatherings.

The Community Appeal. If I were a betting woman, I'd like to make a wager. Taking two churches more or less alike, whether in town or in the country, let one rely on the cook-and-eat plan, while the other releases the women of the church for calling, and in six months compare the two congregations. At the end of that time, according to my experience and observation, a church that believes in giving money and making calls will have more funds for the treasury, and a better standing in the community, than if the women wear themselves out preparing food to keep shingles on the church roof.

The Biblical Basis. That idea of farm women about the Hebrew way of paying the tithe is new to me. It sounds plausible. But I think there must be another side. Through the years I have known many spiritual men and women who gave at least a tenth, with more in the way of thank offerings. These friends were not bitter about other ways of making church money, but in their own experience they tithed not only for the sake of doing good, but also as a means of grace. They learned their lesson from the Bible. I share their conviction that this is God's approved way of financing the women's work of the church. How many exceptions he allows, he alone knows. Every woman or group of women asking his help will receive his guidance.

Although it does not come from the Bible, Kant's old rule gives us a convenient yardstick. In paraphrase it reads: "So live that if everyone else lived your way, this would be a perfect world." If all our women's societies stressed the New Testament idea of trusteeship, and depended mainly, if not wholly, on giving to the Kingdom through the regular channels, what kind of church would we have in every community? In large measure " a glorious church, without spot, or wrinkle, or any such thing." If all women resorted exclusively to other means, what would we have? God only knows. If all our churches kept compromising, what would follow? Confusion worse confounded. It seems to me that we ought to set up the New Testament standard of giving. I am not an oracle. But I plead with my reader to study the Bible, which is inspired, and in the search to follow the guidance of the Holy Spirit.

RELATED READINGS

Depew, A. M., *The Cokesbury Stunt Book.* Abingdon Press, 1953.

Harbin, E. O., *Games of Many Nations.* Abingdon Press, 1954.

Hogan, Bernice, *Abingdon Party Parade.* Abingdon Press, 1954.

Kirk, Jane, *Projects That Pay.* Harper & Brothers, 1953.

Kirk, Jane, *Quantity Cooking for All Occasions.* Fleming H. Revell Co., 1954. Five hundred menus and recipes for all types and sizes of gatherings.

Maguire, Clyde M., *The Cokesbury Dinner and Banquet Book.* Abingdon Press, 1953.

13

AS A TRUSTEE OF GOD'S TREASURE

God loveth a cheerful [hilarious] giver.
— II Cor. 9:7.

L ET US LOOK again at this money matter. Certainly it
is the Lord's business. In all of it he wishes us to be
spiritual, practical, and kind. Many of us think of church
money in terms of the tithe plus thank offerings. If we
could persuade a majority of our church women to give
this way, our treasurer would have a smile beautiful to
see. But we ought not to use a steam roller to crush out
other ways of giving.

USING UNCOMMON WISDOM

During the years of depression some women's groups
had great difficulty in meeting the assigned budget. In
fact, many societies had to default, and consequently all
too much of our mission work had to be curtailed or given
up. At the same time in many churches facing the same
problem, the women " had a mind to work." They gladly
tightened their belts and returned to the sort of thing they
had given up during their plush period.

One society had always raised its budget in full through
voluntary gifts. Seeing that the work faced a deficit, the
leader asked some of her friends to join in serving a series
of suppers. Each time a different group would provide all
the food, and do the cooking, serving, and cleaning up
afterward. The plan worked well. All the money was

163

clear gain for the society. The women who carried the
load had happy times together, and no one toiled long
enough, or often enough, to injure her health or fray her
temper.

However, not all the women were enthusiastic about
breaking the precedent of voluntary giving. But the " out-
siders " kept sweet. They did not hold back or criticize,
and they did all they could to make these suppers a success. Meantime some of them prayed for guidance toward
a better way of meeting that tenacious deficit. At the annual election there was a change of officers. They did not
let the matter of raising money versus giving become an
issue.

Quietly the new leaders went to each member of the
supper committee and asked her a question, which might
have hurt had it not been prompted by a sincere interest.
" Do you remember how much you spent on food for the
suppers last summer? " Every woman did, for in those
days a dime looked bigger than a dollar today, and a
dollar seemed larger than the moon. The number of dollars per hostess ranged from two and a half to ten. With
these facts in hand, the new leaders asked each woman
who had served, " Are you willing to give the same
amount this year? " Every woman agreed to donate the
same sum at a meeting that would be different from anything the society had done so far. The leaders proposed
that anyone who brought ten dollars would be called a
hostess. Two women could become co-hostesses by bringing five dollars each, and four could join at the rate of
two and a half.

The matter was brought up at the next meeting of the
executive board. All the women agreed that it would be
easier to give money than to cook and serve a supper on

a hot night. At a general meeting of the society the president announced a unique "Foodless Supper," and invited the women to become hostesses. The idea took. Some of the men were so relieved that they asked if they might become hosts, and send ten dollars apiece. Perhaps they did not relish having their wives "work out" for money.

The Foodless Supper was held at a private home, out in the garden where the flowers were in bloom. A short program was followed by light refreshments; the hostess provided fruit punch, with nothing in the way of food. When the treasurer had counted all the gifts from the several hostesses and their husbands, she reported a little more than had been earned during the preceding summer.

One objector to the plan said that it suggested how much to give. She spoke for a minority. One of the main group said: "I always felt so mean in not offering to help last summer, but I just was not up to it physically. I am so happy to be a hostess this summer." Not only does some such plan lead to the raising of enough money to prevent the society deficit; the whole enterprise tends to boost the morale of the group.

Another letter recommends a clever plan for a "Diminishing Party." This operates at a large suburban church in the midst of a building program. The women have pledged to carry their regular missionary budget, which is large, and also to furnish the new church kitchen. Down in their hearts they may have determined to show the men how to equip this part of the Lord's house. Let's hear what the leader has to say:

"Our parties created quite a stir in the church. The women had a good time coming to them. This, I feel, is as important as the money. I started by inviting to my home the sixteen women on the executive board. Each of them in turn invited to her home eight other women. Later each of the eight invited four.

" Every hostess planned her own party and program. One had a book review, another a missionary sketch, and some planned only for a social time together. Some of these took the form of teas, or luncheons, and some were evening parties, with husbands present, and light desserts. Whatever plan the hostess used, everyone present gave fifty cents."

The membership lists were parceled out so that each group would include a number of the newer women, and some of the inactive ones, with enough of the regular workers. A few of the inactive ones fell down on the follow-up assignments, but on the whole the plan worked admirably. It got the women of the entire congregation to work together on a project that appealed to everyone. Furthermore, it led to the forming of new friendships and the cementing of older ones. The cost per woman was less than that of a ticket to a movie.

Obviously such a plan would go better in a large church than a small one. The general idea ought to take hold in a group of any size, provided the workers are willing to reach out and enlist all the women not engaged in such work at other churches. The figures below indicate how the plan works, at fifty cents per woman. Actually, at last reports, the total exceeded $500, with a few parties still to be held.

Members of the Executive Board — 16 —	$8.00
Friends of the Sixteen — 16 × 8 —	$64.00
Enlisted by Larger Group — 124 × 4 —	$256.00

SETTING UP OUR GOALS

While we are making or giving money, we should ask what the plan is doing to the women and to the church.

We should keep genuine religious standards in mind, whatever project we have chosen. In the first place, we all agree about the need for promoting *Christian fellowship*. There is something about eating together, visiting together, or just milling around together that makes for a family spirit. In Old Testament times, " they that feared the Lord spake often one to another: and the Lord hearkened, and heard " (Mal. 3:16). Our book of remembrance keeps up to date only when we are in touch with our fellow Christians.

Socials. and teas, luncheons and suppers, dinners and bazaars, all planned and carried out by the women themselves, provide some of the most satisfying ways of meeting this God-given desire to get together and know one another. We come in the name of the Lord, but that does not keep us from having fun. Naturally in church activities we like to have a change of diet once in a while, something refreshing and relaxing, and maybe even a trifle foolish. That helps to keep us normal.

Like Martha, many eager church women get weary in well-doing. The replies to my questions show that the burden of the project method is likely to fall more and more on a few shoulders. As the years go by, the shoulders grow weaker. An aging pastor told his deacons when they suggested a raise in salary: " I'm already humpbacked and bowlegged trying to raise the salary I have. Don't ask me to do any more! " So the women mumble to each other after a bazaar or supper: " I'm dead on my feet." " I'm going to sleep a week." Sometimes their husbands say more, and no mumbling about it! They see no reason why God's work should endanger their wives' health, as human efforts often do by the very breathlessness of our pace. We cannot enjoy each other when we are exhausted. We can take delight in human fellowship when we balance work with sensible recreation.

A second standard ought to have more notice from church women than it usually receives. Every project should be in line with a *definite religious purpose*. For instance, some of the women write: "We are raising funds to buy a car for our missionary in Japan." "We are raising money to beautify our church." "We are doing this to keep a boy and a girl in school in the mountains of Tennessee." The list could be lengthened almost indefinitely, but these few examples show how to reach the hearts of women. If it helps the giver to know where her money is going, it helps her even more to understand the purpose of her giving. Behind and before each project there should be a Christian motive.

Set your standards high, and keep them there.
Make every project definite in time and place.
Tie everything up with a person dear to women.

A third standard should be that of *dignity*. "Whether therefore ye eat, or drink, or whatsoever ye do, do all to the glory of God" (I Cor. 10:31). I have already spoken about amusement, which does all of us good, yet surely a project with a serious purpose need not depend on slapstick comedy or what the advertisers call "cheesecake." Catchpenny games, flippant jokes about sacred things, and an off-the-cuff attitude will never tally with the purposes of the Kingdom. We had better make a different approach when we are working for the church. Every woman should know how to be dignified without seeming as stiff and cold as something halfway thawed out of a deep freeze. In fact, two marks of Christian dignity are personal warmth and radiance. We need these qualities in money-raising projects, as in all our church business.

PROMOTING CHRISTIAN TRUSTEESHIP

Many of these other matters will put themselves right if we set our hearts on promoting trusteeship. In the management of a bank or other financial responsibility, as in handling an estate, a trustee is somebody important. A trustee appointed by a judge considers it an honor. How much more should we consider ourselves honored to be set apart of God to serve as custodians of his church money!

We ought to learn God's will in dealing with the money that we receive from him. As far as we know, the only sort of trusteeship that comes from God, and receives his endorsement, is the tithe plus freewill offerings. I know that Jesus and his disciples did not directly enjoin the paying of a tenth part of one's income to the church; but they seem to have taken it for granted. For ourselves the tenth is only a minimum. A good many of us ought to be giving more. The leaders of the Seventh-Day Adventist Church no longer ask for ten per cent as a minimum; they call for twenty-five. As a consequence the church has abundant funds for its expanding program.

Even if nobody accepts the Hebrew tithe as a binding obligation, we still ought to know what the Old Testament teaches. In words addressed to farming people, a prophet speaks about their need for a renewal of communion with the Lord: " Bring ye all the tithes into the storehouse [the church], that there may be meat in mine house, and prove me now herewith, saith the Lord of hosts, if I will not open you the windows of heaven, and pour you out a blessing, that there shall not be room enough to receive it" (Mal. 3:10). Obviously the Lord doesn't promise that he will make every tither a millionaire, but that he will bless the church whose members offer the tithe out of their love for him.

In Malachi's day not everybody kept the Hebrew law. These careless church members got a biting rebuke: "Will a man rob God? Yet ye have robbed me. But ye say, Wherein have we robbed thee? In tithes and offerings." If anyone spoke that way to a trustee now, those would be "fighting words." In terms of modern church life, what is the Old Testament prophet saying? God has given us everything we have. As church women we wish to use these endowments as a trust. How much does he wish us to give? For some of us there is no escape from the tithe as a minimum, and with many of us, it should be much more.

One woman asks: "How do people compute their tithe? What are the exceptions, if any?" There is a difference of opinion among earnest persons as to where the emphasis rests in this matter. About half of them wish to stress tithes and offerings; others do not want to be "too legalistic."

If a man draws a stated salary, and is honest, he reports this sum to the Government when he makes up his income tax returns. He knows to a penny what one tenth amounts to. Certain exemptions are deductable. Some tithers advocate tithing what is left after the deductions are made; others prefer to tithe the salary as received.

When the income is not paid in stated amounts at regular intervals, the problem is more complicated. My guess is, however, that if a person who has this problem were told he would receive a ten per cent bonus on his income if he could figure out the amount, he would not find it an insuperable difficulty to arrive at a fairly accurate figure. The same computation would decide how much is the

Lord's ten per cent. As for exceptions, if there is any question, give the Lord the benefit of the doubt. It always pays! The motive should never be "the more I give the more I get," but in God's arithmetic that is the way it works out.

Another woman writes: "My husband handles most of the money at our house. He has a large salary and pays all the bills. I have only a small allowance from him for spending money. How can I pay the tithe?" Indeed, how can she? If I had such a husband I would — well, perhaps I should not say what I would do, but I am sure I would "speak to him" about the matter. A man who asks a woman to bear his name, rear his children, and make a comfortable home for him, and then gives that woman a measly allowance is a stinker! Perhaps he thinks he is "protecting" her from unpleasant experiences with tradesmen. I am glad to believe, however, that the number of such husbands is small, although I have known one or two of that breed.

In a Christian home the money is usually divided on a 50–50 basis between husband and wife, with a clear understanding about the financial responsibilities each has to carry. If this is done, there need be no trouble about computing the tenth part.

Still another woman inquires, "Is it right to give a part of one's tithe to other good causes outside the church?" Definitely, yes. The Red Cross, Community Chest, Y.M.C.A., Y.W.C.A., Christian colleges, hospitals, etc., all have a legitimate claim on the Lord's money. We prefer in our family to give the larger portion of our tithe through regular church channels, but we also support these other benevolent organizations with the tithe. When that runs out, then there are freewill offerings. "If any man will do his will, he shall *know* " (John 7:17).

The Children of Israel were expected to give the tithe for what we call local church support. They did not then reach out in what we know as missions. Neither did they have the example of the cross, and the outpouring of the Holy Spirit. In the light of Calvary and Pentecost should we not expect more from ourselves in the way of giving than from those who lived on the other side of the cross and the resurrection? Instead of being bound by law, we are free, free to give far more than the ancient Hebrews. Today there is only one strong argument against the tithe as a minimum. As one schoolteacher reports: " I tried it for a while, but I found it cost more than I wanted to give up. I need the money myself."

Wherever church women have given themselves, and along with their lives have contributed the tithe and free-will offerings, the Lord has blessed both givers and gifts. But we must never make the tithe a substitute for other, deeper things in religion. Jesus warns the Pharisees, " Ye pay tithes of mint and anise and cummin, and have omitted the weightier matters of the law, judgment, mercy, and faith: these ought ye to have done, and not to leave the other undone " (Matt. 23:23). Woe unto you, twentieth century hypocrite or Pharisee, who makes the rustling of dollar bills a gesture of pious fraud!

There is a difference between a pose and the real thing in giving to the church. The following is from a member of a businesswomen's group, among people with middle-class incomes. " When I first joined this society, I was amazed at what a group of women can do when they take part in what is going on. Our group is composed of twenty-five members, most of them active. Our thank offering this year is over $600.00. When extra donations are asked for, the girls go 'all out.' The thank offering is over and above our regular budget for missions."

A tithe giver finds this habit a sort of benediction. In a Christian sense your dedicated money means you. Through the tithe your influence reaches out as far as your prayers, helping to transform human destinies. If once you adopt this way of serving the Lord, and follow the plan in the spirit of liberality, you will thank God for permitting you to serve as a trustee of his manifold grace.

"'O Lord, how much?' we inquire.

"Jesus answers, 'All.' He asks for all or nothing, with no irritable quibbling over less or more. God's grace is costly; so is human faith. If you render to God what belongs to him, it will cost you your life. From that complete investment will flow lesser gifts to nourish the life of the church."

MEETING OBJECTIONS KINDLY

In time every tithe payer ought to become a "home missionary" promoter of trusteeship. In the South we lived a mile from a church where thirty-eight of the forty-two officers and teachers in the Bible school were enthusiastic tithers, and a similar proportion among the members of the Christian Endeavor. While not large, the congregation had a community influence that extended far beyond its bounds. The reason for the number and ratio of tithers among the officers and people traced back to the example of one person. Only a few years before, this person had become an apostle of trusteeship through the tithe and thank offering, and had persuaded others of its value. The entire church felt the impulse of regular, systematic, and proportionate giving.

The advocate of tithing must know how to meet objections in a kindly spirit, but without compromise. The efficient promoter doesn't waste breath arguing. Even if she meets a belligerent sister whose conscience pinches, the one who believes in trusteeship keeps on smiling. Instead of getting drawn into an argument, she can refer to a case or two, let the subject drop, and pray that the good seed will bring its harvest in time. The two examples that follow come from life. The first of them we heard from a minister who related the facts out of his own experience, and the other came through a conversation I can vouch for.

When the late Bishop Edwin H. Hughes was a young man, he served for a while as pastor of a Methodist rural church in the Middle West. One day in preaching he said that we own nothing; it all belongs to God. Following the service a farmer took the minister home for dinner, and after a sumptuous meal the two men walked out to see the broad acres of farm land, with all that was on them. The farmer showed the parson spacious buildings, new equipment, sleek cattle, and many other evidences of prosperity. Then he said:

" My wife and I started here without a dime from anybody else. We have worked and saved and bought everything you see here. If we don't own this farm, who does? " The young minister replied in a kind tone of voice, " Will you ask me that question one hundred years from today? " Once in a parable our Lord said much the same thing to a rich farmer who did not reckon on tomorrow. " Then whose shall those things be, which thou hast provided? So is he that layeth up treasure for himself, and is not rich toward God " (Luke 12:20, 21).

The second case has to do with a woman, also in a rural community of the Middle West. A group of seminary seniors were lying out under the trees talking of their lifework, soon to begin actively. One of them said that he wanted to promote the tithe. Another protested, "I don't think it's fair to the widow and her orphans." The best man in the group smiled, and told this experience:

"My mother was left a widow with five children, the oldest of us in his early teens. My father had been a home missionary. He never had much money, and my mother had nothing when he died but a small farm. We moved out there. One day Mother called us older children and said that she wanted to talk things over with us. When Father was living we had always paid the tithe. When he left us, Mother quit. But she told us, 'Now I want to begin again.' It looked as if we were heading for the poorhouse, and we told her so. Well, she told us if we did go there, she wanted to go with a clear conscience. Yet she said that God would take care of us. She believed it. And it wasn't long before we felt that way too. All I can say is that I feel God has blessed our family. I don't mean *because* we paid the tithe — but Mother kept us together, saw that all of us had a good education and became active in the church. You can say that tithing isn't fair to widows and orphans, but we never felt that way at home."

With these human interest examples in mind, let us think of tithing as a kind of trusteeship, and giving as a means of showing our gratitude to God. According to the Bible, "God so loved . . . that he gave," and we want to become deserving of such a Heavenly Father. We do not feel superior to women whose lot has been less favorable than our own, but still we enjoy privileges and benefits that many of them would like to have. Therefore out of gratitude and humility we should continue to work hard, save as we go along, and give as the Lord has prospered us. The work of our society will flourish. Perhaps in later years sons and daughters of the church will enter Christian vocations, partly because their mothers have set them an example of Christian trusteeship. At heart this means giving ourselves first, and then our substance. "I seek not yours, but you" (II Cor. 12:14).

Some of us here at home have never yet learned what it means to give. We ought to ponder these heart-searching words from D. T. Niles, missionary of India: "We who are Christians are too flabby in our interests. We have time for everything for which those who are not dedicated to the cause of Jesus have time. We have money to spare for all the things that others surround their lives with. And we are hoping to seek and to serve the Kingdom with spare money in spare time. It can't be done."

RELATED READINGS

Cushman, Ralph S., *I Have a Stewardship*. Abingdon Press, 1946.

Grindstaff, W. E., *Developing a Giving Church*. Fleming H. Revell Co., 1954. A prominent Baptist leader stresses the tithe and other means of raising money.

Harrell, Costen J., *Stewardship and the Tithe*. Abingdon Press, 1953.

Jordan, G. Curtis, *What Are You Worth?* Bethany Press, 1954.

McRae, Glenn, *Teaching Christian Stewardship*. Bethany Press, 1954.

Rolston, Holmes, *Stewardship in the New Testament Church*. John Knox Press, 1946.

Zuver, Dudley, *She Did Take It with Her*. Harper & Brothers, 1954.

14

AS AN EXAMPLE OF CHRISTIAN LOVE

So faith, hope, love abide, these three;
but the greatest of these is love.
— I Cor. 13:13 (R.S.V.).

I F I HAD to make a decision that would affect me or anyone dependent on me, if ever I were in difficulty or
distress of any sort, I would go straight to Queen Mary."
So said a woman who had lived close to the queen for
years, though she was not of the same royal rank. This
woman was saying that she found in Queen Mary a friend
whom anyone would love and the sympathetic wisdom
that anyone could trust. Similarly, a woman's faith gives
her confidence in the never-failing love of God.

BEING A REAL CHRISTIAN

Replies to the questionnaires indicate that church leaders and pastors keep on the lookout for this kind of
woman. One of them writes: "The key to success in
women's work is I Cor., ch. 13 — love." A pastor says:
"True humility is hard to keep pure. But without this
mind of Christ there can be no love in its purest form.
This is the greatest need in our churches today." Another
pastor adds, "Our emphasis is on fellowship in Christ,
rather than just getting things done." To be a real Christian, one must know the love of God in Christ.

The reports go on to say: "We discover fresh talent by
using new women in some small work, such as serving on
a committee. If they get along with people, then we shove

them into office and really work them. We try to develop both diplomats and ambassadors for Christ. We avoid like leprosy the women who take themselves too seriously, and ponderously walk about loaded down with the luggage of self-love." Other reporters agree on the necessity of love and humility; they feel that the two belong together in us — as in Christ. Since we are earthen vessels, as church women we must often be aware of our deficiencies, but we need not give up and become weepy about them. Rather let us look honestly at ourselves and ask what went wrong. "Where did I fail? How could I have done better? Why do I feel upset because things didn't go my way? Was the other woman's plan so much better than mine? The majority seemed to think so." Thank God for the mirror on the wall; it tells the truth. So does the mirror of fearless self-criticism.

Someone says that the secret of a happy marriage is to treat disasters as incidents and not to treat incidents as disasters. The same rule holds good in women's work. We are inclined to balk at trifles, and to skip lightly past the things that matter most. What William James has written about " a certain blindness in human beings " applies to church workers. We often see faults and shortcomings in others, but we never suspect the same traits in ourselves. A real person makes the most of her own blessings, without attempting to regulate all the human race.

Such interest in people appears in the writings of the late Dorothy Dix, well-known columnist and confidante of women. Her biography offers ten rules for a happy life.

1. Make up your mind to be happy.
2. Make the best of your lot.
3. Don't take yourself too seriously.
4. Don't take other people too seriously.

5. Don't borrow trouble. [And don't lend it!]

6. Don't cherish enmities and grudges.

7. Keep in circulation, with many interests, many friends.

8. Don't hold post-mortems, brooding over mistakes.

9. Do something for somebody less fortunate.

10. Keep busy.

These words sound like ten echoes from Philippians. Any Christian woman wants to make the most of her God-given abilities, and still not seem like a plaster saint. If you begin to fret because you haven't developed into an efficient, imaginative church leader in a month's time, perhaps you need a prescription that Frances Willard once compounded as a cure for discouragement: " Take one teaspoonful of pleasant memories and three teaspoonfuls of forgetfulness of sorrow. Mix well with one pint of cheerfulness. Take a portion every hour of the day." As a busy leader of women, " she made it a rule never to answer a letter or give an opinion until she had brought herself to feel charitable toward all the parties concerned." She would have agreed with Mahatma Gandhi: " When you are right you can afford to keep your temper and when you are wrong you cannot afford to lose it."

In all of life " love is the fulfilling of the law." According to D. T. Niles, personal goodness comes best through a sense of being loved. " In my home I do not live as a person under obligation to love my wife and children. I live as a person who is loved by them. My wife does not live as a person under obligation to love me and the children. She lives as the object of our love. The children do not get up in the morning saying, ' We must love Father and Mother.' They simply live in the consciousness that they are loved." Isn't this a religious parable? We cannot generate love in our own hearts, for love has only one source, and that source is God. No recipe book can give us the actual ingredients of love. God alone can do that. The real Christian experiences God's love in Christ, and makes it effective in everyday living.

KEEPING HER DAILY APPOINTMENT

Sooner or later every Christian woman discovers that her inner life consists in patiently nurturing and constantly checking a soul that will reach perfection only in heaven. No amount of church attendance or taking part in group worship can be a substitute for the normal and balanced life of personal devotion. That is one of many reasons for a woman to keep her daily appointment with God. Evelyn Underhill declares: " All the great masters of worship insist on the importance of the secret personal life of adoration as ' the first essential for a Christian.' . . . For it is the self-oblivious gaze, the patient and disciplined attention to God, which deepens understanding, nourishes humility and love; and, by the gentle processes of growth, gradually brings the creature into that perfect dedication to His purpose which is the essence of the worshiping life."

The replies to my letter reveal that our women have many different ways of meeting with God in the " quiet watch." One friend suggests daily use of the hymnal in the time of prayer. You may begin with such words as " Holy Spirit, Truth divine, dawn upon this soul of mine." If you decide to use the hymnal, buy your own copy, and do *not* borrow one from the pew rack in the church. Find a song you know and love — likely it will be a prayer hymn. For variety search out other hymns that you do not already know, and learn them by heart. You will find a treasury of worship in these songs. All in all, one of the best books for personal devotion is the Protestant hymnal.

Other friends follow the practical suggestions in *Today*, *The Upper Room*, or some other booklet that supplies daily light and inspiration. Most churches distribute these worship aids. One invalid of long years says that she feels lost without her devotional guidebook.

For these helps we give thanks, but I recommend first of all, and most of all, the Bible itself. Among educators there is a growing sense that many of their troubles have come from the grasshopper curriculum, scrappy survey courses, books about books, and a nervous leaping from topic to topic. Does not the same generally hold true of Protestant devotional life? One is hardly expected to stay with a given book of the Bible long enough to learn its message or feel its impact. Yet this Book, which offers the wisdom of God and the power of God, invites one to a steady companionship. Such intimacy cannot come by snipping a text here today, another there tomorrow, but only by a steady, continually deepening friendship with a Person.

In my businesswomen's class we had finished reading the Gospel According to Luke. One of the members said to me: "That is the first time in my life I ever went through a whole book in the Bible. Why, Luke stands out like a cameo from all the rest of the books!" I daresay that this young woman confessed what others in the class were thinking to themselves. It is important to remember that the average church today has in it scores of people who have never sat down and read through a whole book of the Bible. A Bible class or women's group should encourage the individual to find in Scripture new dimensions for Christian love.

Many devout women follow the general course of the Christian Year. Starting after Thanksgiving, they read in Isaiah, and in Luke or Matthew, about the way God prepared for the coming of Christ. After Christmas they read one of the Gospels. After Easter they turn to the book of The Acts or one of the Epistles. After Pentecost they look to The Psalms or a historical book of the Old Testament. Briefly, interests change with the changing year.

During the time of meditation do not try to study the Bible. This is not to counsel that " it pays to be ignorant." Study has its importance, especially for a teacher in the church school, but knowing the distance between Dan and Beer-sheba is, after all, not quite the same thing as knowing God. As you read, reflect. A certain verse in its context will reach out and grip you. Memorize it along with the hymn. Mark it with a pencil, and if you read the passage at an hour when the words have particular significance, such as at a time of grief, write the date in the margin. By so doing you will be setting landmarks in your spiritual autobiography.

In private meditations you can devote half the time to Bible-reading and the other half to prayer, but let these two activities be intermingled. As an aid in the most difficult part of personal devotions many women follow *The Book of Common Prayer,* or some other guide filled with the best that saints and martyrs have uttered in supplication to God. And yet for personal meaning the prayers of the ages will never supplant your prayer for today.

DEALING WITH WANDERING THOUGHTS

" Why can't I think about God for three minutes at a stretch? " Wanderings of mind may cause you searchings of heart, but some morning you will make a glad discovery. " God cares about everything that concerns me. If my mind wanders — well, so can my prayers. With my Heavenly Father I am just like my little girl. She shifts from one thing to another, and comes up with the most unexpected questions. I know that she loves me and wants me to love her, and that's why she tells me about the things that look important in her life. Isn't prayer the same — talking things over with a loving Father? " Think of your prayer as conversation, and don't even try to pray as your pastor does in church. Public worship and private devotions have entirely different settings, and should therefore take different forms.

A regular hour helps you to pray. A woman can talk things over with God while sorting the clothes or darning the boys' socks, and I recommend it, but she should also have a time and place reserved for prayer and devotional reading. The hour must fit into the daily schedule, and the place may be determined by the arrangement of the house. These matters are adjustable, yet if a woman keeps her Bible near at hand, opens it and reads from it at about the same time every day, her thoughts will naturally be led Godward. All of us do best what we have a time and place for doing.

Some women advocate praying aloud. This does not mean speaking so that you can be heard in the next room, but using actual words and complete sentences as a means of uttering thoughts and feelings. What begins as a disposition to let your thoughts wander may thus become an intelligent, persevering, and well-directed habit.

Moreover, specific prayer helps to fix attention. Pray for individuals. Thank God for definite blessings. Ask him to provide what you want most for today, the actual desires of your heart. A dear friend used to " fuss and sput-

ter" over things when they went wrong. Her husband
would say, "Turn your worries over to God, dear, that's
what he is for." Another friend objects, "I don't believe
in bothering the Lord every time the bread doesn't rise."
Well, I do! I have often prayed over a meal, both before
and after serving it. My days — and yours too, I imagine —
are a mosaic of details. We do well to pray about the arrangement of the bits that make up the total picture.

> "O what peace we often forfeit,
> O what needless pain we bear,
> All because we do not carry
> Everything to God in prayer!"

Unless one is watchful, private devotions may become
as automatic as counting beads. Day after day one utters
the same petitions for the same persons, until one can
prattle the words without thinking. As a guard against such
mockery a woman may use the missionary prayer guide
issued by her denomination. Another person who is quite
original prepares her own list of persons at home and
abroad for whom she wishes to pray. As new needs arise
among her friends or in the work that fills her thoughts,
she adds those names to the list and prays for them.
When prayer has been answered, she gives thanks as she
makes an erasure from the list. In fact, a woman's prayer
list, and the way she uses it, provides a fairly accurate
index of her spiritual life.

In his diary John Wesley wrote: "I resolved, *Deo
juvante*, (1) to devote an hour morning and evening to
private prayer, no pretense and no excuse whatever;
(2) to converse with God; no lightness, no foolish talking."
Few of us give that much of the day or night to secret
devotions, but if we spent more hours in prayer and used
the time as Wesley did, we too might grow in Christian

love, and in the power to do more work, better work, glorious work.

GETTING OTHER WOMEN TO PRAY

All that I have been saying illustrates my belief that group worship and the inward life of faith go hand in hand, each supporting and strengthening the other. Several pastors mention a new emphasis on prayer groups among women. Sometimes these groups are known as cells. Each cell gathers around a woman who has learned to pray. In one of these prayer fellowships the members covenant to read and pray at home, giving special attention to a suggested list of books and the church school lesson for each coming Sunday. When the number of women in a cell grows too large, one of them starts a new cell in her neighborhood.

In many societies all the circle leaders follow the same plan, by using some book that pilots them toward " their desired haven." The leaders link their Bible-reading with a particular need or problem in our time. For example, turn to The Book of Ruth in the Old Testament. The story of Ruth and Naomi brings up the question of how we treat the modern immigrant. The facts about Ruth the Moabitess, in direct line of our Lord's ancestry, stimulate thoughts for prayer about uprooted people today. Or turn again to Genesis and read about Sarah and Hagar, whose relationship strikingly suggests the recent Jewish-Arab tensions in Palestine. How much do we think or pray about these plagues that come back to us like the return of locusts?

Devotional leaders may come together a few days before their circles meet, to study the lesson with the spiritual life secretary, or, if he has the time and is willing, with the pastor. In her letter to circle leaders, one woman who is in charge of the study tells them, "We dare not come to our groups unprepared." She assigns the passages for study and gives pointers on what to look for. In quiet trysts at home the devotional leaders become familiar with the Bible passages, getting ready to talk about them in the circle meetings. The following excerpt from a letter to her circle leaders shows that the Bible is a contemporary book, full of fascination for women:

"Barbed wires and bombs in Jerusalem! What do they stem from? Do they stir the dust in the fields of ancient Judah? Do the children of Sarah and Hagar now war and wound each other with weapons of which these old-time women never dreamed?"

Group devotions ought to lead every woman who takes part in them toward the horizon — and beyond. As Margaret Applegarth says, Christians ought at various times to pray for "all Africans and Alaskans, all Burmese and Brazilians, all Danes and Dutch, all Chinese and Chileans, all French and Fijians, all Hottentots and Hindus — until you run out of letters but not out of names, so immense is God's rosary of saints and sinners, all equally dear to him."

When women pray fervently and unitedly, a blessing comes to the church. A strong difference of opinion was threatening to split a city congregation. Things had come to a deadlock. The official board appealed to the Prayer Fellowship for help at the throne of grace. The women met and prayed for "the peace and prosperity of Zion." They never had prayed with such beseeching earnestness. They claimed Christ's promise that "if two of you shall agree on earth as touching any thing that they shall ask, it shall be done for them of my Father which is in heaven"

(Matt. 18:19). At the congregational meeting there was lively debate, but no bitterness and no open rupture. The dissenters agreed to go along with the majority, and from that day onward the work of the church prospered because there was peace. One of the leaders among the men attributes the victory of faith to the prayers of these women. "Prayer directed by consecrated women," he writes, "makes things happen. The spirit of harmony and the unanimity that prevail are conclusive evidences of the power and efficacy of united prayer."

Here the work had begun to develop through the efforts of one woman, more than ten years before, who had led her friends in praying together. In an old-time missionary society, small and not well organized, she had invited a few interested women to her home during Lent. They sat around the open grate fire, reading the Scriptures and uniting in spoken prayer, with periods for silent meditation. Later on, when all the women's organizations in the church came together in a single body, the same spirit of devotion prevailed. While still in the "toddling stage" the leaders wanted to give the Bible a central place in every circle meeting. There were murmurs of dissent, especially from the pie-versus-cake debaters who belong to every such group, but by loving persistence the women kept the Bible and prayer at the heart of their work. With these two focuses, round which everything else revolves, the society now engages in a wide variety of good works.

In this large congregation the stress does not fall on bigness, complexity, or statistics. There is rather a sense of reality when the women have a quiet moment "for confession of careless work, easy excuses for inefficiency, and putting other things before the 'one thing needful.'" At the same time there is a sense of power in their willingness to be led by the Holy Spirit. As a result of a devotional attitude the number of workers and the range of their activities have kept increasing year by year. In the early days of the Prayer Fellowship eight or ten women attended faithfully; as their influence has spread, the numbers have grown as well, and today they can count on one hundred women to respond to a call for prayer.

The reporter concludes: " As we review the accomplishments of the years not one of our early group now feels that the results have been due to anything she has done. Everyone rejoices that the Lord has chosen to work through her in answer to prayer. These all agree that it has been a glorious experience to witness the growth of their work under the guidance of the Holy Spirit, who releases his power in response to united prayer."

In a small town in Texas lived a humble Christian woman who exerted a strong influence, not only in her own home, but also out in the community. She would go quietly to one whom she knew not to be a professing Christian, and in her patient, yet persuasive, way she would instruct and guide that one, through the reading of the Bible and earnest prayer, until she had led him to the light.

During a revival meeting the evangelist asked the people one night to go and shake hands with the one who had brought them to Christ, if that person were present. More than twenty men and women clustered around this gentle little woman to testify that it was through her counsel and prayers that they had been led to Christ.

At some future time our children will judge whether our years of patient and often exhausting effort have strengthened the Church at home and overseas. Doubtless, too, they will carry on the Lord's work in ways different from those we now use, just as we have changed the methods that our mothers once employed. But one thing is certain: As long as the Church is the Church, there will be one clear channel for learning God's will for its life, the channel of prayer; the one inexhaustible power for winning souls to him, the power of Christian love.

"In short, God has chosen to employ prayer as his means of transforming men and nations. All the while the power rests with him, not in us or in our prayers. So let us give thanks because he has placed in our hands a power mightier by far than any number of atomic bombs. 'This is the victory that overcometh the world, even our faith.' "

To serve as a leader among church women you don't have to be a brilliant organizer or an eloquent speaker, but you do need to know God's love in Christ. That is the indispensable element. "So faith, hope, love abide, these three, but the greatest of these is love."